LOVING
CREATION

Advance Praise for *Loving Creation*

"In the midst of our current global crisis, Fischer presents an ecological spirituality that is insightful and compelling. Sustained commitment to caring for the universe, she insists, must be motivated by a genuine love of creation, for we will not labor to save what we do not love. In this inspiring call to healing our relationship with the natural world, Fischer makes clear that loving God requires loving the earth, for the divine Spirit abides in all things. Her holistic approach applies the wisdom of Christian spirituality to ecological concerns in creative and refreshing ways, showing clearly how our tradition contains indispensable resources for an ongoing care of the earth."

Wilkie Au, author of *By Way of the Heart:*
Toward a Holistic Christian Spirituality

"We need to find new ways to live and new understandings of our place on the planet and in the wider universe. Fischer's book is a reliable guide to this necessary work of discovery and reevaluation."

Rich Heffern, author of *Daybreak Within:*
Living in a Sacred World and *Adventures in Simple Living*

"As she traces the relationship between Christian tradition and ecology, Kathleen Fischer offers a fresh view of owning our roots in the earth. She brings to life the perennial values of reverence, compassion, gratitude, and positive asceticism. Once again she has shown herself to be a gifted and sensitive guide in the journey to integrate body, mind, and spirit."

Jane Kopas, author of *Sacred Identity: Exploring a*
Theology of the Person and *Seeking the Hidden God*

LOVING
CREATION

Christian Spirituality, Earth-Centered and Just

Kathleen Fischer

Paulist Press
New York/ Mahwah, NJ

Cover and book design by Sharyn Banks
Copyright © 2009 by Kathleen Fischer
Cover photo © by Anita DeFina Hadley

Library of Congress Cataloging-in-Publication Data

Fischer, Kathleen R., 1940–
    Loving creation : Christian spirituality, earth-centered and just / Kathleen Fischer.
        p. cm.
    Includes bibliographical references (p.   ).
    ISBN 978-0-8091-4603-1 (alk. paper)
    1. Human ecology—Religious aspects—Catholic Church. I. Title.
    BX1795.H82F57 2009
    261.8′8—dc22

                                                                    2009027249

Published by Paulist Press
997 Macarthur Boulevard
Mahwah, New Jersey 07430

www.paulistpress.com

Printed and bound in the
United States of America

CONTENTS

Contents

PREFACE

The house in which I grew up was built of brown shingles and planted on an acreage in Keizer, Oregon. Its five tiny rooms were far too small to hold our family of nine, so my brothers, sisters, and I lived mainly outdoors. We chased butterflies and grasshoppers, climbed cherry and apple trees, and gathered handfuls of the pink and blue cornflowers that grew wild in the surrounding fields. It was to nature that I first turned for solace and strength, there that I learned to look for grace in the rumpled life emerging from hatched eggs, in the metamorphosis of watermelon seeds, and in the inviting fragrance of wild roses.

Before I knew the inside of a classroom, I was familiar with the lessons of strawberries and raspberries, filberts and pole beans, for from the time I was five I helped harvest the many crops that flourished in the rich soil of the Willamette Valley. I was innocent, however, about the nature of pesticides. My siblings and I ingested them on the berries we surreptitiously ate while filling our crates, and shook them from the beans that filled the sacks we lugged to the scales to determine our day's earnings. Only later did I learn about the impact of pesticides on the insects, plants, and land we cherished, and on our own developing bodies.

Many who love creation have had similar experiences of finding the sacred in nature but gradually awakening to how seriously we are endangering life on our planet. During the last half-century, religious thinkers, along with those from many other disciplines such as science and economics, have probed the causes of our ecological crisis and proposed ways to address it. Because of their pioneering work, we now have a growing well of wisdom from which to draw, an ever expanding theoretical base to guide us. We also have the inspiration provided by religious leaders from a variety of faith traditions. In his 1990 World Day of Peace Message, Pope John Paul II declared the ecological crisis to be a moral problem of such proportions that it has become everyone's responsibility.

In spite of this ever expanding base of knowledge and exhortation, it remains challenging to move from theory to practice, to find ways to infuse our lived faith with a love of creation. For this shift involves more than making efforts to recycle, searching for new energy sources, and reducing carbon footprints—essential as are such research and actions. What is asked of us cuts even closer to the core. It calls us to a whole new way of living in the universe, a transformation perhaps greater than we have yet begun to imagine. As scientists themselves have acknowledged, saving our planet turns on a fresh spiritual vision and the practices that flow from it.

Many sense the need for this redirection. Greed, selfishness, and violence do exist, and they make headlines each day in our media. But the women and men I talk with every day want to do what is right for our planet and its inhabitants. They embrace with enthusiasm the new cosmic story and stand in awe at the immense and complex creation it reveals. They grieve the desecration of the Earth and the loss of precious species. They worry about the kind of future their children and grandchildren—and all future generations—will inherit. But at times they are paralyzed by the sheer enormity of the problem. Or they relegate ecological concerns to the future while they struggle with immediate and pressing issues such as medical diagnoses, teenagers on drugs, financial worries, family conflicts, and caring for those with physical or mental illness. I hope to show that what seem to be personal and private concerns are intertwined with the well-being of the Earth.

As appeals for saving our planet become increasingly urgent, we all stand in need of support and encouragement, lest the changes asked of us appear overwhelming and take us to despair. In light of this challenge, my goal is to show that Christian spirituality—its sacramental vision, biblical traditions of inheritance and promise, ancient prayer practices, saints and prophets, teachings on desire and asceticism—offers indispensable resources for converting our hearts and minds while sustaining our hope. We discover, perhaps to our surprise, that an ecological perspective, rather than residing at the edges as a special category of spirituality, belongs at the center of Christian faith.

I begin this work of integration with a meditation on our creation in the image of God, since divine and human images constitute the matrix of any spirituality. The fact that we dwell with a relational God in an interdependent cosmos changes, in fundamental ways, how we understand spiritual maturity. Next I explore a sacramental vision of the universe and the unique value of each species, perspectives that ground our efforts to save all living beings. Subsequent chapters address the intrinsic connection between ecological concerns and work for peace and justice and the central role of the emotions and the imagination in conversion. Jesus' dream of the reign of God serves as a beacon throughout, illumining our dark nights and reminding us that the God who creates is also the God who redeems.

These ancient and new spiritual perspectives make clear that the series of transformations we need for this critical time on Earth—the required changes in worldview, lifestyle, and action—comes ultimately as God's gift. Our part is to make ourselves available to grace. I therefore include suggestions for ways to pray with the chapter themes; others will no doubt arise from your own reflection, prayer, and conversation.

If you wish to read more about some of the topics I treat, a section of notes and further reading offers suggestions for pursuing particular issues in greater depth. For those of you who have already made ecological concerns part of your daily spiritual practice, my hope is that this book will deepen your awareness and strengthen your resolve. If the plight of our planet has not yet moved you, may this book create for you a whole new vision.

CHAPTER 1

WHO WE ARE MEANT TO BE

We must be ready to surrender to the process of transformation ahead of us; eager, or at least willing, to appropriate the patterns of the Beloved Sophia and move with the earth toward greater variety, intensity, and depth of expression.

—Constance FitzGerald

Certain moments awaken us to the universe in which we live. Perhaps a total lunar eclipse—a full orange moon suspended in a star-studded sky, with the bright planet Saturn nearby—evokes wonder at our vast and complex cosmos. We try to imagine over a hundred billion galaxies still hurtling farther apart, each with a hundred billion stars. Or we study an image taken from space of our blue marble Earth, a small but beautiful planet from the spiral arm of the Milky Way Galaxy. A seamless community of life stretches across Earth's circular surface.

If we look close up at any part of this home planet, we find it buzzing with intricate and dynamic forms of life—mites and millipedes, bacteria and fungi, beetles and sparrows, horses and cottonwoods. Probing further, we learn that this immense and complex universe began with the explosion about fourteen billion years ago of a dense and hot fireball. From this primordial bit of matter/energy came all that we see around us—galaxies, stars, planets, human beings, and other creatures. We share the same ancestry as all other beings in the universe, and are intimately linked with them; we are all made from stardust, formed from the atoms of galactic explosions.

As this contemplation deepens and expands, central questions for Christian spirituality come into sharp relief: What does spiritual maturity look like in such a universe? Can we still anchor our identity in the biblical belief that we are made in the image of God? How shall we name the divine spark shining at the heart of creation? This historical moment adds a special urgency to our answers. Stemming the damage we are inflicting on our planet requires that we consider anew how we are made in the image of God, how we share in the divine creativity. Fortunately, abundant resources exist for understanding who we are meant to be.

ALL CREATION AS IMAGE OF GOD

An ancient tradition tells us that human beings, male and female, are made "in the image of God" (Gen 1:27). These opening passages of the Bible also invest humans with dominion over the rest of creation—the fish in the sea, the birds in the air, plants, animals. But this creation story has come under scrutiny in recent decades amid concern that it depicts human beings as the peak of creation with divine permission to dominate it, thus contributing significantly to our current ecological crisis. Alternate interpretations of the creation stories stress that we bear the divine likeness not in subduing nature, but by being responsible stewards of it and by living in kinship with other creatures. Other themes also illumine our imaging of God: the delight God takes in everything created, pronouncing it "very good"; the description, in the second creation narrative, of the newly created human beings as placed in the garden to "till it and keep it"; and the sabbath rest in which all creation culminates. On the seventh day, the entire Earth community celebrates God's presence with creation. A day of blessing, a time for all creation to pause and simply be what it is meant to be, the sabbath points to full companionship rather than any single species as creation's climax (Gen 1:31—2:3).

In spite of these other motifs in the Genesis accounts, the industrialized world has used control as its primary template for humanity's relationship to the natural world. First we mastered fire, air, water, and atomic power, and now with technological and scientific advances, the extent of this domination appears to have no limits. But the consequences of this approach to nature have become clear. Like cancer, uncontrolled mastery metastasizes, poisoning and depleting its host. Recognition of the price domination exacts has contributed to a search for new understandings of the divine spark that defines us.

Attempts to interpret the *imago Dei* in ways that honor the integrity of the entire creation have moved beyond the Genesis narratives to mine other rich veins of the tradition. The biblical wisdom writings offer one such resource. For some decades now the image of God as Sophia or Wisdom has quietly taken hold in spirituality. At first she was totally hidden, and then tentatively embraced as an alternative to exclusively male imaging of the

Divine. Now, variously called Holy Wisdom, the Wisdom Woman, or Sophia, she has entered more fully into prayer and theological discussion.

Wisdom literature does not separate the Creator from the world, but holds the two in tension. Proverbs and the Wisdom of Solomon portray Sophia as the love that brings the universe into union. She takes account of the potential of all that is created, enlivening and energizing everything.

> For you love all things that exist,
> and detest none of the things that you have made,
> for you would not have made anything if you had
> hated it.
> How would anything have endured if you had not
> willed it?
> Or how would anything not called forth by you have
> been preserved?
> You spare all things, for they are yours, O Lord, you
> who love the living.
> For your immortal spirit is in all things.
> (Wis 11:24—12:1)

Something of an artist always lives on in her works. Made in God's image, all creation holds up a mirror in which we glimpse traces of the divine beauty and holiness.

Reflected back to us, this image shapes our sense of who we are. When Sophia alters our vision of reality, we perceive that every species is known and valued for itself, as it is in God. We not only find God in the world, but the world in God. As the sixteenth-century mystic John of the Cross exclaimed: "These mountains—my Beloved is this to me! These valleys—my Beloved is this to me!" When we meet Sophia in prayer, we no longer see ourselves as divided from other species, for we find our connections in her. Sophia teaches us to love the Earth and delight in it as she does. In "Hagia Sophia," Thomas Merton writes of the way the Divine dwells in all the forms of creation, shining "not on them but from within them." Other creatures live out their likeness to the Divine in the very forms of their being. Each aspect of creation praises God by becoming what it is called to be.

If Sophia cares for all creatures, then the importance of human beings cannot be established at the expense of the rest of creation. Wisdom reaches from one end of the universe to the other, pervading and ordering everything (Wis 8:1); she shows creatures their beauty and possibilities. When each finds its own inner truth, all together create mutual ways of living on our planet. Wisdom's ways are not the usual exploitation and competition. She stands right at the very highways and crossroads of the world and there calls us to transformation: "To you, O people, I call, / and my cry is to all that live" (Prov 8:4). The voice of Wisdom must be heard today in these public places where global decisions are made about the quality of our soil, water, and air, "for she teaches self-control and prudence, / justice and courage" (Wis 8:7).

The New Testament writers, especially Matthew, John, and Paul, tell us that the Wisdom that creates the universe is the Wisdom revealed in Jesus. As ecological theologian Denis Edwards notes, in light of all that we know today, this would mean that the Wisdom made flesh in Jesus is an endlessly creative word, "the Word of the Big Bang, the primordial hydrogen, star formation, the Milky Way Galaxy, planet Earth, bacteria, clams, frogs, and chimpanzees." New Testament hymns and epistles describe Jesus in terms used for Sophia, as the one through whom all things were created (1 Cor 8:6) and as the image of the invisible God (Col 1:15). Like Wisdom, Jesus invites those who are burdened to find rest in him (Matt 11:28–30); he turns people into friends of God and infuses those who love him with life (John 17:2). He asks us to envision a web of relationships that embraces even our enemies. Just as Jesus is the image or icon of God, so we are meant to become by grace what he is.

If each creature displays Sophia's creative order and patterning, and matters uniquely to her, then we are to respect the wisdom of the many species who share the planet with us, honoring their habitats, their ways of survival and play, their unique modes of communication, their emotional lives, and their special intelligences for swimming and flying, mating and migrating. Ecological thinker Mary Evelyn Tucker insists we are to cherish and protect these processes: "That is why the movements of animals and birds, fish and insects were so carefully observed by earlier peoples who recognized their dependence on these creatures and celebrated their closeness to them in song and painting, myth and dance." Though we no longer dispute the fact that other creatures can think, we have scarcely begun to decipher their ways of knowing and being known, and their singular languages.

Uniqueness, as seen in the context of mutual care, allows us to appreciate other species' differences from us and ours from them, as well as what each needs to survive and thrive. The moral philosopher Mary Midgley describes our ethical obligations as determined by the multiple memberships we hold in both human and nonhuman communities. It is, she believes, our duty to remember the many gifts we have received and the small part we play in "a vast, irreplaceable and fragile whole." Because human self-realization is more complex than that of plants and animals, we are called to values that are rooted in wisdom. We experience intricate emotional states and forms of language, countless variations on the themes and expression of anger, joy, love, and fear. We are meant to live with compassion and justice in ways not available to species that operate simply out of instinct and need. We also fail to fulfill our calling in ways that birds and bears, tulips and rivers do not.

Kinship with other creatures involves us in complicated interactions with plants and animals as we exchange energy with them and participate in the food chain that sustains us all. This web of kinship is no romantic notion, but marked by the sacrifice one life form makes for the survival of another, by the many deaths that generate new life. Here in the Pacific Northwest that cycle is vividly present to us in the salmon that swim upstream to spawn, dying soon afterward and providing food for eagles and bears, and nutrients for the forests and streams that will nurture the next generation.

A TRINITARIAN IMAGE OF GOD

The Trinity embraced by Christian faith sometimes seems an abstract notion, suggesting speculation on a divine inner life that is beyond our knowing and theological controversy that holds little relevance for daily decisions. Belief in the Trinity, however, has clear implications for how we view creation and define human uniqueness. The early Christians did not try to probe God's inner relations; they knew the Trinity first from the way salvation came to them—as God's action in the Word who was made flesh, and in the Spirit whose saving gifts were poured out on them. Later generations then began to question what this experience says about God.

What emerges from this history of theological reflection is an image of God as radically related, a communion of love and equality, giving and receiving, that preserves and enhances the unique gifts of each person. Theologian Catherine Mowry LaCugna believes that a revitalized understanding of trinitarian theology should free our imaginations, showing us that the heart of God is to be in relationship and that in God there is no room for hierarchy, inequality, or divisions. The trinitarian relations reveal the kind of emptying out that makes room for the *other*. Understanding God in trinitarian terms establishes the basis for creation's dignity within a richly differentiated unity. The Greek word for the pattern of mutual interrelationships in the Trinity is *perichoresis*, a movement of love between the three persons that flows outward to the world. In creation, this divine intimacy is freely shared with all creatures. Denis Edwards comments that *perichoresis* is close to, although distinct from, a word that means "to dance around the other." He nevertheless finds the dance an apt image for the divine relationships that dynamically nourish and sustain creation.

Taking seriously this *imago Trinitatis*, our creation in the image of the Trinity, subverts our individualistic notion of reality, thus changing the way we experience everything in the cosmos. If creation reflects the mutual indwelling of the Trinity, then the dead zones in the Pacific Ocean that are lacking oxygen, the hillsides denuded of trees, the battered child in Africa, the poor and oppressed throughout the world are part of our body. They reveal to us our own violence. One way of expressing this communion that constitutes creation is to speak of the world as God's body. God is in the world and the world is in God—the world and all who dwell in it are the bodily expression of the divine communion.

The cultural historian Thomas Berry believes that even in its very cellular structure, its freedom, communion, and diversity, the universe mirrors the Trinity. He is convinced that we need to develop a feeling for the universe "as subjects to be communed with, not objects to be explained." Since seeing ourselves in communion with other human beings is itself a stretch, however, extending this to the rest of creation—animals, plants, water, air, mountains, and fields—requires an even more supple imagination. Our efforts stumble when we try to think in this new way, since most of us in Western nations have from childhood named ourselves as though we existed as isolated individuals—separate place settings, separate rooms, single-occupancy cars. We believe that we first become a person, and then focus on relationships as a secondary level of thought and action.

In fact, relationships are constitutive of who we are, not later additions. We are made from everything that exists; life is a gift from other beings, not only at birth, but throughout our existence. As poet and essayist Susan Griffin writes: "I know I am made from the earth, as my mother's hands were made from the earth, as her dreams." Griffin's words echo the second Genesis creation account where God forms humans, along with all other life, from "the dust of the ground" (Gen 2:7); in this passage, all living beings arise from the same topsoil.

Every aspect of creation is in some sense both subject and object, part of a stream of mutual exchange. To say that we are constituted by our relationships is to acknowledge the presence and power of other beings in our becoming. We are sometimes aware of this in terms of a friend or teacher whose influence continues to be felt in our lives long after the initial contact. This is another way of expressing the fact that relations are not external but internal to who we are. They are not accidental, like a change of wardrobe; rather, they actually become a part of us. We experience this most vividly when a person we love dies, when we lose a beloved pet, or when we find a dead whale washed up on the shore. We feel that a part of us has died with them, and in fact the way they live on in us has now changed. Past forms of presence have been transformed into something new.

How then, within this fabric of mutual intimacy, are we to understand human uniqueness and calling? An amazing variety of species makes up the Earth community, each with its own special characteristics. Human beings, like all species, are most certainly unique—different from rocks and volcanoes, mosquitoes and giraffes. The human sciences have located this singularity in a combination of attributes, none proving sufficient in itself: emotional subtlety, abstract reasoning, imagination, play, myth, art, self-awareness. Religious traditions have grounded human dignity in our creation in the image of God. Throughout history this divine likeness has been identified with many different aspects of the human person—the soul, reason, freedom.

Many ecological theologians today situate human uniqueness in the power of self-reflection. Although consciousness is present throughout creation, in human beings it reaches its fullest expression. Since we are part of creation, in loving other beings we are retrieving lost parts of ourselves. Rather than being in or on the Earth, we are that part of creation that is most fully aware of itself and responsible for directing its evolution. Years of working with persons who have Alzheimer's disease or other forms of dementia make me hesitant to find the image of God exclusively in self-reflection. For when persons with dementia lose self-awareness, they are still fully persons, able to relate in other ways. As a therapist, it is also clear to me that models of the human that stress awareness discourage rather than inspire those struggling with various physical and emotional limitations.

If we are made in the image of a trinitarian God, then our uniqueness may reside in the capacity for mutual relationship. As theologian Catherine Keller asks, "To decide for the most heterogeneous width of relations that I in my edgy finitude can embrace—is that my creativity in *imago dei?*" Is it then my responsibility to take as many of these relationships as possible into account when I make a decision? The strongest and most creative love consists in a mutual giving and receiving. The wisdom needed for our time of ecological concern will then arise from reciprocal and creative relationships, from the kind of communion that shapes and directs our energies rather than from efforts to control and master nature. As we listen and learn from all of nature, the true good of all will gradually emerge.

This power of love stands in contrast with the power of domination. Conceiving of power as love recognizes that receiving the influence of other beings in the universe requires even more strength than exerting influence. Love readies us to take into account as wide as possible a span of the feelings and values of all beings. Jesus excelled in this kind of power, opening himself to those living outside the realm of established authority—tax collectors, sinners, the poor, the blind, the lame, the sick, prostitutes. He was affected by all of them, and he reached back in love to each. We are asked to use the size of his love as the measure for our presence in the universe: "I pray that you may have the power to comprehend, with all the saints, what is the breadth and length and height and depth, and to know the love of Christ that surpasses knowledge, so that you may be filled with all the fullness of God" (Eph 3:18–19). Jesus rejected all forms of domination and power over others (Mark 10:42–45); so must we.

The divine creativity dwelling in our families, cities, races, and genders has potential to widen and deepen the sense of community that grounds our decisions. Within its broader horizons, we continually learn ways to reverence both nonhuman and human nature. Only from within this altered perspective can we find our way to collaboration in the complicated issues that care of creation entails. In the Northwest this has meant seeking solutions that somehow honor loggers and their families as well as owls, old-growth forests, and rivers. A report on efforts to save African wildlife makes this point. The most successful conservation programs in Africa are premised on people's needs: "All we have to do to preserve Africa's wildlife heritage is care about the people as much as we care about the wildlife." Within the fundamental connection between humanity and nature such issues can be approached in ways that combine social justice and ecological concern, that honor both the rights of all species and human rights.

THE IMAGE OF GOD AS PROMISE

Contemporary science reveals a universe that is unfinished, marked by unpredictability and promise. The new arises repeatedly and in many ways. The matter of the very early universe transformed itself into new states, then clusters of galaxies, individual galaxies, massive stars, condensed dust particles, and planets. Nature surprises us repeatedly with the emergence of the unexpected, showing us a creation that is far more dynamic than we realized. Yet beginnings do not determine the course or final state of the self-organizing processes of creation. As the astrophysicist Arnold Benz comments: "To be sure, a human being bears the old within, but is something quite different, something qualitatively new." The cycle of death and resurrection appearing in both small and great ways in nature provides a pattern of promise—of present and future hope.

We know in faith that the Creator Spirit has been with creation from the beginning, a mighty wind sweeping over the face of the waters (Gen 1:2), moving in each burst of life that unites the past with future possibilities. The Spirit is the dynamic flow of divine love sustaining the universe, bringing forth life at every moment. Throughout creation we find spontaneity or freedom, but also mysterious patterns that pervade the cosmos and our own becoming. In the final book of the Bible, God says: "See, I am making all things new" (Rev 21:5).

This Spirit, present at the heart of creation from its beginning, works gently, taking into account where creatures are at every point. Like an artist who builds on previous sketches or imprints, the next touch of the Divine relates to all that has gone before. The Spirit dances and takes chances, sends creation forth on adventures. The mathematician and philosopher Alfred North Whitehead speaks of this divine initiative as the poet's lure that sets in motion all becoming and movement in the universe. It is directed to the flourishing of the entire Earth community. Just as a poet draws out our response by presenting a compelling vision of reality, so God exercises tender patience in leading us to the divine vision of truth, beauty, and goodness. It is this Divine Poet, God as Companion, who fosters compassion in redistributing the goods of the Earth, and creativity in pursuing peace and harmony for future people, plants, and animals.

God's image in us, however, remains an ember waiting to burst into flame. We dwell in a universe of fractured relationships where the Spirit longs to breathe the Pentecost tongues of fire into full form. We are asked to see the *others* in our midst as they are, not as we expect or want them to be; dealing with differences is neither simple nor easy. Intimate connections with family and friends feel frayed, weakened by conflicts and misunderstandings. Mutuality is blocked by hatred and violence in local and larger communities. Trafficking in women and children fuels a major industry, and many human beings around the globe are treated as objects rather than free subjects. Creation groans under the burdens we have placed upon it. Communion remains an unrealized ideal. We therefore know the *imago Dei* as promise and hope as we share the Spirit's yearning for a world where the Earth and all its inhabitants will abide in reconciliation and justice.

Although the image of God in us remains unfinished, as individuals and as communities we are being shaped even now by the Spirit into the pattern of Christ. This Spirit transfigures all the relationships that are ugly, shameful, diseased, hurt, and broken. A key aspect of our participation in this new patterning is receptivity to the God who continually pours out love to all creation, calling us forward into what we are meant to be. When we remain long enough in the presence of someone who loves us, we become what we find in that person's gaze. Their image of us is engraved in our heart, burned into our being. So does God's vision for who we can be abide in us, continually influencing who we are and what we do.

An ancient understanding of the Spirit as the bond of charity that unites the Father and Son in trinitarian love reminds us of her power in healing the self's divisions of mind and heart, as well as all the splits and dualisms of public life. The Spirit's love crosses the boundaries that breed hatred and violence, pressing for dialogue in the midst of religious, gender, racial, and class differences. The environmental justice activist Mark Wallace suggests that we think of the Spirit in our time as a wounded Spirit who takes into herself the burdens of human sin and ecological damage. The Spirit does not remove her presence from the planet, but pours out God's love for all that is earthly and bodily. Her agony is a source of hope, as she repeatedly offers us the opportunity to change, continually bringing life to creation in spite of our death-dealing behaviors.

Encountering the *other*—whether in family, church, or society—carries with it a bracing challenge, how to be enriched rather than threatened by difference. Both grace and sin are social as well as personal realities. We take heart from knowing that just as every act of hatred weakens in some way the threads that bind us as one, so too every act of love strengthens the cosmos. Spiritual maturity does not consist therefore in striving for individual perfection or in solitary self-scrutiny, but in the messy and chaotic process of relating to others and finding ourselves through these relationships. We become like God when we widen the size of what we are able to include and embrace, and join with the Spirit who sustains communion.

The Spirit is at work transfiguring the power of domination into the power that is love. Love in such a perspective is not the attempt to connect with others. We do not become related when we love one another; we are already related. In a universe that is in process of becoming, we are not free to choose *that* we will be related, but we choose *how* we will relate, that is, whether our relationships will be characterized by love or hate, healing or destruction, fear or trust. The process of healing brings about a change in *how* a relationship exists in our lives—as an endless source of sadness, fear, and resentment, or as integrated somehow into the self in a new way.

This healing of relationships has often been limited in the past to the interpersonal; now it extends to the Earth. What is the state of the threads of receiving and giving that bind us to the web of all beings, to soil and sky, sandpipers and whales, beetles and blossoms? Does the energy of these relations reflect the love of the Spirit, or are we blocking its movement by our refusal to care? What of our links to future generations of plants, animals, and human beings? Is our use of natural resources honoring their needs? The healing of relationships extends to all these larger systems.

A full sabbath celebration of creation lies still in the future, as the hope toward which all creation is moving. The meaning of sabbath develops in situations of oppression and liberation. Later biblical writers emphasize that the sabbath is meant for all—the cattle, the land, the Earth itself; human beings, including women, children, and slaves (Exod 23:10–11; Lev 25:1–7; Deut 5: 12–15). Letting the fields lie fallow teaches the people to live in harmony with the land and give thanks for its blessings. As the Israelites wander in the wilderness on their exodus from Egypt to the Promised Land, God declares a sabbath during which the people are to cease their efforts to secure bread, for God has freely nourished them (Exod 16:22–30). Just as the Genesis passage moves from chaos to sabbath, so here, the people move from frantic feelings of anger to quiet trust, from a chaotic insecurity to contentment. For all sojourners, sabbath rest emerges in wilderness, in the place where sustenance is received as gift, and security arises from trust in God's future care.

Restoring the sabbath to creation calls a halt to the productivity from which the Earth knows no relief, from global transactions that operate around the clock. Sabbath days or moments secure a silence that reveals the meaning of existence beyond work and activity, a pause that honors the grace that brings all toil to fruition. In these quiet intervals we can let the *imago Dei* embed itself ever more deeply in our hearts and imaginations. Rhythmically repeating short prayers, matching them to the movement of our breath, allows the meaning of creation in the divine image to resonate within us. Choose one of these, or fashion your own brief prayer.

> Sophia sings in all creation.
> Our Creator calls us to communion.
> Creator Spirit, you pervade all relations.
> Teach us to dwell in your wisdom, Sophia.
> Spirit of love, heal our Earth.
> Dancing Trinity, unite us in You.

Made in God's image, we celebrate on sabbath the divine vision of a mutually life-giving community, one in which all beings sustain one another in joy and suffering and anticipate the future in hope.

CHAPTER 2

WE WILL SAVE
WHAT WE LOVE

The Spirit of God is a life that bestows life
root of the world-tree and wind in its branches.
She is glistening life alluring all praise
all-awakening, all-resurrecting.

—Hildegard of Bingen

Late one cold December afternoon my husband Tom and I decided to walk an area overlooking Puget Sound called Magnolia Bluff. Clear skies and a steady breeze created perfect conditions for a display of Northwest splendor. To the south, Mount Rainier appeared in snow-capped splendor, and to the west stood the entire Olympic range, its peaks also dusted with recent snowfall. Beneath these mountain ranges the setting sun appeared as a fiery ball of orange and red, and then, like a silk scarf unfurled, it swirled across the sky in streams of red, pink, yellow, and orange. Bathed in its color, tug and sailboats plied the waters. As the sun's hues began to recede, a newly full moon, ringed with its own circle of light, climbed the eastern sky. On the street, passengers from two tourist buses emerged transfixed, their cameras trained on the scene.

Though accustomed to finding our area beautiful, we were stunned by this panorama, and Tom exclaimed: "What colors are here! Who painted this?" These moments at the edge of the Sound were for us a sacrament, a visible manifestation of the God "in whom we live and move and have our being" (Acts 17:28). A sacramental vision of creation, the belief that the Divine lies hidden in even the most ordinary aspects of life, forms the foundation of Christian spirituality. It prepares us to encounter the sacred in all things—the biblical word, the depths of the self, the complexity of relationships, the rituals of community, the immensity and intricacy of the cosmos.

Of these sacramental realities, it is the natural world that concerns us now. Early and medieval theologians—Bonaventure, Hildegard of Bingen, Thomas Aquinas—saw nature as a path to knowing God and frequently included it in their theological reflections. Nature was considered a book of revelation. In his preaching, Augustine spoke of the two books God has given us, the book of Scripture and the book of nature. If we learn to read the book of nature, he believed, we will hear God's word and grow in our understanding of the Divine.

Many who are concerned for the future of our planet, both theologians and scientists, fear we have lost this sense of nature's holiness, thus paving the way for the Earth's destruction. Thomas Berry notes a certain futility in efforts to remedy ecological problems simply by reducing the impact of the industrial world, for example, by seeking alternate energy sources. These approaches, though intelligent and necessary, still view nature primarily as an object of human use, a commodity to be bought and sold rather than a sacred reality to be approached in veneration, wonder, and intimacy.

Ultimately we will save only what we love, what we reverence as sacred. How can Christian spirituality contribute to a revived sense that the entire universe is sacramental? How fire the imagination to see the natural world with new eyes? We will explore several avenues for lifting into awareness this dimension of the tradition.

THE SACRAMENT OF THE COSMOS

In their efforts to recover the religious significance of nature, a number of contemporary thinkers have returned to the work of the Jesuit paleontologist and religious thinker Pierre Teilhard de Chardin. In the last months before his death on Easter of 1955, Teilhard remarked that he was still attempting to express the same fundamental vision he had laid out in *The Divine Milieu* and "The Mass on the World." Both works reveal the profoundly sacramental character of his vision: "The great mystery of Christianity is not exactly the appearance, but the transparence, of God in the universe." He believed that the Divine pervades the entire cosmos.

The matrix of Teilhard's thinking was World War I, during which he served as a stretcher bearer. From the outbreak of the war until the end of 1918 he experienced his first extensive contacts with ordinary working people and also had time for intense reflection and prayer among the arching columns of trees near the Aisne River in France. In the midst of the horrors of war— the trenches, the exploding shrapnel—Teilhard discerned the energy of love straining toward greater communion. The thirteen essays he wrote during this period attest to Teilhard's passionate commitment to the energies and hopes of the Earth and to his equally strong dedication to the Divine. His effort to discover the connection between these two realities—faith and science, God and the universe—governed his thinking.

In *The Divine Milieu* Teilhard situates the Christian totally within the network of the physical world, participating in it fully as milieu, womb, and source of self. But the world is a divine as well as human milieu, since Christ constitutes its meaningful center and animating goal. Teilhard's spiritual vision emphasizes the importance of the forces of passivity, failure, disease, and death as well as those of activity. He balances attachment with the profound detachment inseparable from creative effort.

A central question absorbed Teilhard: whether the Christ of the gospels who is imagined and loved within the dimensions of a Mediterranean world can embrace an immensely expanded universe. In the cosmic Christ, Teilhard found the resolution to his dilemma. He was convinced that Christ's redemption extends to a creation as expansive as the whole cosmos: "Christ is all and in all!" (Col 3:11). He quotes Colossians 1:17 often—"He himself is before all things, and in him all things hold together"—and 1 Corinthians 15:28 even more frequently: "...so that God may be all in all." The risen Jesus provides the center and focal point for the cosmos, drawing all things to himself. In our own small ways of moving the universe forward toward universal love, we contribute to this reconciliation of all things in Christ.

Teilhard's mysticism expressed itself in an extension of the Eucharist to the entire creation. The sacramental transformation of bread that occurs in the Eucharist becomes for him the paradigm of the universal transformation of the material world. During a scientific expedition in the Ordos Desert in 1923, when Teilhard found it impossible to offer Mass on the feast of the Transfiguration, he turned to the radiation of the eucharistic presence of Christ throughout the universe. Moved by all he observed around him, Teilhard made the Earth the altar on which he offered the world's growth and diminishment.

The meditation that resulted, "The Mass on the World," relates the parts of the liturgy of the Mass to God's presence in the material world and to our participation in that divinized world. His prayer encourages us to imagine how the deepest meaning of the Eucharist relates to our current ecological crisis: "Over every living thing which is to spring up, to grow, to flower, to ripen during this day say again the words: This is my Body. And over every death-force which waits in readiness to corrode, to wither, to cut down, speak again your commanding words which express the supreme mystery of faith: This is my Blood." In this prayer, Teilhard reminds us that in each of our eucharistic celebrations, we too lift up all of creation, asking that it be transformed by the Spirit into the body of Christ. In the Eucharist we are called to bear in mind that bread and wine are the fruits of the earth and the work of human hands. Since humans are intrinsically connected to all else in the universe, when we come to the table, we somehow bring all other creatures with us as well.

Teilhard's "Mass on the World" captures the central Christian belief that the Eucharist is meant to transform existence. In all of the sacraments the ordinary things of life—water, words, the breaking of bread, the sharing of a cup of wine, touching with oil—take us into the Christian mystery. The sacraments regard physical reality with ultimate seriousness and ground our responsibility to care for the Earth. As the central celebration of a sacramental people, the Eucharist provides a fundamental starting point for an ecological spirituality. It opens us to the divine presence found in all food, friendship, water, light, and darkness. Alive to the Eucharist's cosmic meaning, we begin to recognize that the entire universe—air, sky, soil, animals, plants, and people—makes possible our continued becoming.

Because the sacraments link us to matter everywhere, the water and oil that are a part of their ritual action connect us to oil spills in Alaska or San Francisco Bay, to wars over the world's oil supplies, and to seas polluted by the world's waste. Their symbolism extends as well into all our table gatherings, making a sacramental vision of the Earth the theme of the grace we say before meals.

> We gather here before gifts of the land and treasures of the sea.
> We thank the Creator Spirit for the Earth's blessings.
> We bless the creatures of field and farm who feed us with their lives.
> We join in praise of the Divine Love that holds us all in cosmic communion.
> May our sharing in this food and drink keep us aware of our dependence on all beings for life and strength.
> May it increase our reverence for land, sea, and sky.

ATTUNEMENT TO THE RHYTHMS OF THE NATURAL WORLD

A recovery of Celtic monasticism and its traditions of prayer also enriches our search for God in the physical world. The ancient Celtic countries of Ireland, Scotland, Wales, the Isle of Man, Cornwall, and Brittany lay for the most part outside the boundaries of the Roman Empire and its influence. They were therefore free to develop a distinctive spirituality. Their blessings, poems, prayers, and songs were handed down orally and collected in Scotland and Ireland at the end of the last century.

A rural people, the Celts remained close to the earth and the elemental aspects of the material world—stone, fire, sea, wind, water, sun. They discovered there a God of both companionship and sheltering presence. One of the oldest Celtic prayers, "St. Patrick's Breastplate," captures this experience of nature.

I arise today
through the strength of heaven, light of sun,
Radiance of moon,
Splendor of fire,
Speed of lightning,
Swiftness of wind,
Depth of sea,
Stability of earth,
Firmness of rock.

As seen in this prayer, Celtic spirituality invokes the ordinary rhythms of human life from birth to death—getting up, washing, making a fire, fishing and farming, going to bed. But it also includes the divine voice speaking in all of creation from dawn to dusk and season to season. Moreover, this prayer calls on all the senses, making it bodily in a full and intense way. For example, an invocation at rising asks for God's blessing on all to be encountered during the day, ending with a quiet reference to the Trinity.

Bless to me, O God,
    Each thing mine eye sees;
Bless to me, O God,
    Each sound mine ear hears;
Bless to me, O God,
    Each odour that goes to my nostrils;
Bless to me, O God,

Each taste that goes to my lips,
Each note that goes to my song,
Each ray that guides my way,
Each thing I pursue,
Each lure that tempts my will,
The zeal that seeks my living soul,
The Three that seek my heart,
The zeal that seeks my living soul,
The Three that seek my heart.

The Celtic Christian tradition holds that God speaks in both the Bible and creation. Drawing especially from the wisdom literature of the Hebrew Scriptures and the Gospel of John, Celtic spirituality finds the divine image embedded deep within all living beings. Enduring, as they did, the harshness of poverty, discomfort, and demanding physical labor, they did not minimize suffering or whitewash the fierce and destructive patterns of nature, even as they praised its extraordinary beauty.

The Celtic people learned from the monasteries the spirituality that infused their ordinary life, including the ideal of continuous prayer. Later monastic tradition also contributes to our attunement to nature's rhythms. Benedict instructed his monks to treat the land and the tools of their work as they did the vessels of the altar. In this way he instilled a sense of devotion toward material things, and participation in the shape and rhythm of divine time.

The Liturgy of the Hours and the seasons of the Christian liturgical year carry on this celebration of the cosmos and its rhythms. In the Easter Vigil the proclamation of creation as sacrament reaches a climax. The *Exsultet* or Easter Proclamation summons all creation to be delighted, all the Earth to find joy in the resurrection. The cosmos continues to share in this Easter exultation as the fire and the paschal candle are blessed, the

Genesis creation account is proclaimed, and the waters are prepared for the newly baptized. All creation bears this Easter light and hope into the world's dark places.

POETRY AS TEXT FOR PRAYER

The story is told of how the Talmudic sage Rabbah bar Bar Hana, while traveling in the wilderness of Sinai in the third century, met an old Arab merchant. He learned that the merchant could determine just how far it was to the nearest water simply by taking up sand and smelling it. To see if this was indeed true, the rabbi tested him, first with sand that was eight parasangs (about thirty-two miles) from the nearest oasis, and then with sand that was three parasangs away. But though the rabbi tried to fool him in each case with sand he had substituted from another place, the old Arab proved infallible in his sense of smell.

Intimate knowledge of realities such as sand flows from the mindfulness practiced by contemplatives, scientists, and poets. Certain poets attend to the natural world in ways that show us how to view it with a sacramental lens. Their poetry reveals the sacred center that sustains each living thing and offers us a text for ecological prayer. Many poets evoke this sacred quality of life, but three interest us here: Jane Kenyon, Gerard Manley Hopkins, and Pattiann Rogers.

Jane Kenyon's poetry is based on attention to what she called the *luminous particular*. She saw the art of poetry as a cry of the spirit, musical and brief. Most of her poetry was written from a New Hampshire farmhouse where she could observe winter's full moon, the birth of a calf, fat spiders, matted grasses, and frozen ponds. Deep meditations on the ordinary, Kenyon's poems relate the smallest elements of creation—a hen flinging a pebble, a wasp in the eaves, the porcelain lip of a gravy boat, moments of melancholy—to our largest beliefs and emotions. Particular things are seen as vessels of grace, as in this line from "Now That We Live": "Sky at night like an open well."

At times Kenyon's poems are infused with both spiritual longing and psychic pain. She battled serious depression throughout her life and died in April 1995 after a fifteen-month struggle with leukemia. Her faith was often marked by anguish and doubt, causing light and shadow to alternate in her poems. Yet creation offered her solace in the midst of doubts about its Creator. Through images linked with intense emotion, Kenyon's poetry allows us to share this love and empathy for creation. Finally she felt able to embrace the intertwined beauty and suffering of reality, and this assurance appears in her poem "Let Evening Come," with its refusal to let fear overcome trust in God's comforting presence.

A poet well known for his sacramental vision, the nineteenth-century Jesuit Gerard Manley Hopkins wrote during the Industrial Revolution in Great Britain. His poem "God's Grandeur" asks us to see again the way God's presence flames out, "like shining from shook foil." But he was also troubled by how we cover up that divine beauty, leaving a weary world "seared with trade." Yet Hopkins found the Divine to be only partially hidden, and his poems reveal the glory of its manifestations.

Hopkins's term for the individual form of things, their unique reality, was *inscape*. In the beauty of persons or nature we glimpse the indwelling of God, their inner energy or *instress*. Without this divine presence, there would be no individual reality. Instress often appears as a kind of illumination, a sudden apprehension of the deeper pattern that gives meaning to the external form of a thing. In his journal Hopkins wrote: "I do not think I have ever seen anything more beautiful than the bluebell

I have been looking at. I know the beauty of our Lord by it. Its inscape is mixed of strength and grace, like an ash tree."

In poem after poem Hopkins reaches for the Spirit's energy that makes things alive and lovely as thrush's wings, racing lambs, azure hills, plotted landscapes, skylarks. He expresses the truth found in the poetry of the twelfth-century Rhineland theologian Hildegard of Bingen, that God's Spirit stirs "everything into quickness with a certain invisible life which sustains all."

We find a similar attention to the detailed patterns of nature in the work of the Colorado poet Pattiann Rogers. In October 1997, Rogers visited Olympia, Washington, for a reading. In an interview on her drive from Oregon, she talked about her poetry. Asked about the way she delights in spatial relationships, as in her poem "The Importance of the Whale in the Field of Iris," Rogers said that it gives her pleasure to stir everything up in order to look at reality in atypical ways. Her poems are playful, as with the iris remembering the whale and adjusting its leaves to look like rows of whalebone, or the whale breathing the memory of the iris inside itself. But she believes the poems show us what happens when we break free of dichotomies like body and soul, spirit and flesh, day and night, animal and vegetable, to think in a different way.

Rogers weaves biological, botanical, and zoological details—the flight of a chickadee, cast-off autumn leaves—into dense and witty poems that explore the physical world and the Divine. In "Counting What the Cactus Contains," we ponder its "seven thousand thorns, each a water slide."

In the poem "In General," Rogers takes us in turn through the myriad forms of rain, night, and wind, offering such rich detail that we are nearly overwhelmed by the wealth of images. Each stanza might make a season's meditations. Rogers says that she thinks increasingly of a poem as a piece of music—a hymn, a jig, a waltz—and perhaps that is how we should experience them as well.

Rogers laments that, like previous generations, we do not understand the universe. We have not had time to take the new information the sciences have brought us and incorporate it into a spirituality to live by, one that will enable us to exercise restraint and to act in constructive rather than destructive ways. The arts such as poetry, she believes, can interpret this scientific information in ways that will sustain us. That is what she hopes her poetry will do.

How do we pray the texts of poets such as Kenyon, Hopkins, and Rogers? Poetry changes our awareness, enables us to name and celebrate previously unnoticed aspects of nature, shows us how much there is to marvel at, and helps us identify more fully with the natural world. As we pray with poets' texts, we await the ways God might move in us, how an encounter with fresh images will grace and illumine our perceptions. Poetic metaphors make a link that was not there before, an imaginative leap that incorporates nature into our spiritual world from a new perspective. Our own role consists in opening up and slowing down enough for this to happen. As with other prayer, we ready ourselves for God's presence, however it might arrive. Like the fourteenth-century English mystic Julian of Norwich, who found the whole of God's creation in a hazelnut, we learn to find in the simplest aspects of nature a starting point for prayer.

We might choose to read slowly a poem, silently or out loud, pausing to let its lines linger. Or stay with one image, allowing our imagination to expand or modify it. Memorizing a single line or carrying a line or image from a poem with us through the day sharpens our attention as well. With nature poems it helps to read them outdoors, for example, taking Hopkins's "Pied Beauty" or "Hurrahing in Harvest" with us for a walk or a sitting meditation to see what resonances they stir in landscapes and creatures around us, stopping and listening for the Depth at the heart of matter. Miracles may emerge, but nature's violence, darkness, and struggle—also aspects of mystery—may appear as well.

I have asked participants in a retreat to read a poem silently and let it wash over them, pausing where a line or an image creates an especially strong response. Then, in a prayerful atmosphere of listening, each person in the group speaks out loud one image or phrase from the poem so that these images move freely through the group. The prayer concludes with one person reading the entire poem out loud. As in the biblical psalms, repetition deepens and clarifies the prayer.

Poets instill in us a capacity for contemplation, for taking a longer look at the mystery in which we are embedded. We can find space for this even in the midst of our urban and technological landscapes, and in doing so, we discover the poet in ourselves. In May 2007, the award-winning sports journalist Steve Rushin delivered the commencement address at Marquette University. Toward the end of his remarks he described how just the week before, he and his wife had purchased a new TV set. After unpacking it, they set the box that the TV came in on its side out in the yard so that their two-year-old daughter could play in it. When their daughter, Siobhan, invited Rushin into the box, he joined her and they lay on their stomachs staring for a long time out at their garden. Rushin says that as he and his daughter gazed at the dozens of tulips his wife had planted in rows the previous fall, he began to ponder. He noticed that as the tulips bloomed, they tilted ever so slightly toward the sun. How remarkable, he thought, that in nature, life wants to grow toward the light.

CHAPTER 3

The Worth of
a Single Sparrow

The forms and individual characters of living and
growing things, of inanimate beings, of animals and
flowers and all nature, constitute their holiness in the
sight of God.

—Thomas Merton

One evening this past spring, my husband and I heard a
cacophony of calls from frogs mating in the creek near our home.
We rejoiced at this evidence that yet another species was returning to the area, the latest victory in a project begun on a cold
February morning seven years earlier—the restoration of a natural habitat. Site of an urban creek, the city block had become a
magnet for used tires, abandoned refrigerators, and empty beer
cans and soda bottles. With the help of a city grant, we organized

volunteers to clear and weed the banks, cart in mulch and lay jute, and then plant and water bare-root native plants. Now thimbleberry and Oregon grape feed robins and red-winged blackbirds, and red alder and Pacific madrona trees tower over the growing number of butterflies, snails, and spiders that have returned.

The restoration of habitats is one way we participate in the repair of creation and preserve its biodiversity for future generations. Scientists tell us that we are losing twenty thousand species annually, the largest extinction since that of the dinosaurs sixty-five million years ago. Suddenly a sense of urgency colors efforts once dismissed as the preoccupation of environmentalists with salmon and spotted owls. And our actions do matter. Because of extensive hunting and loss of wetlands, the trumpeter swan was once reduced to fewer than one hundred birds in the continental United States, plus a few thousand in Canada and Alaska. Now, as a result of conservation efforts, it numbers thirty-four thousand. We have prevented a parable of divine beauty and grace from vanishing.

The Hebrew prophets spoke of a famine of the word of God in their time, and today the silenced voice of extinct species threatens to deplete the abundance of God's revelation. The Spirit of God dwells in each creature, allowing it to become a window to the Divine. When creation's diversity thins, this image of God is diminished, like a mosaic with missing pieces. What does Christian spirituality bring to the effort to reverse this species extinction and preserve God's gift of biodiversity? At several levels it supports attitudes and actions essential to the reverence and preservation owed each being in the universe.

THE INTRINSIC VALUE OF ALL CREATURES

We are accustomed to viewing nature as a backdrop for human activity, a subtext to the human story. Young boys who visit the habitat near our home often regard its beehives, for example, as mere collector's items, not as another creature's home. But fresh exploration of certain biblical passages underscores the intrinsic goodness and value of every creature. The Book of Job witnesses to the significance of nature on its own terms by articulating the value of all forms of life independent of their relationship to human desires and needs. Each is a beloved aspect of God's creation. This message becomes especially clear in the book's final chapters, as Job demands an accounting from God for the suffering he has endured, and God responds by pointing in detail to an amazingly diverse universe.

This final sweeping summary in the Book of Job differs from creation's depiction in the first chapter of Genesis where human beings occupy center stage. In Genesis' first creation story, God surveys all he has made and finds it very good, but the divine creative activity appears to culminate in human beings, with all else provided mainly for their benefit. In contrast, the author of Job, a book that belongs to biblical wisdom literature, moves humans to the periphery. God celebrates every aspect of creation for itself, and honors each as evidence of divine grace. Human beings are one of an astonishing array of creatures made and sustained by a divine discernment impossible to wholly fathom. God questions Job:

> "Is it by your wisdom that the hawk soars,
> and spreads its wings towards the south?
> Is it at your command that the eagle mounts up
> and makes its nest on high?
> It lives on the rock and makes its home
> in the fastness of the rocky crag.
> From there it spies the prey;
> its eyes see it from far away.

Its young ones suck up blood;
and where the slain are, there it is."
(39:26–30)

This parade of wonders stands in contrast to the human focus of the rest of Scripture. Viewed in amazing detail, over long vistas, and in cosmic proportions, we see the value of nature independent of human use. With Job we are asked to stand in awe at the grandeur of creation—the constellations, the raven and lion, mountain goats, the wild ass and ox. Further, descriptions of the powerful land animal Behemoth, whose bones are like metal bars, and of the sea creature Leviathan, who spews flames and smoke, undercut human notions of being the ruler of land and sea creatures.

When Job seeks an explanation for his suffering, his friends hold out the traditional reward and punishment view that fails to satisfy him. He can find no meaning even in the covenant. But as he undertakes an imaginary journey through creation, Job begins to see that it reveals an answer to his questions that lies beyond the logic of good and evil, reward and punishment. The ostrich lays its eggs on the ground though they risk being crushed. Behemoth and Leviathan are both monsters, yet they exist as part of creation. He now sees and understands, having participated in creation in a new way: "I had heard of you by the hearing of the ear, but now my eye sees you; therefore I despise myself and repent in dust and ashes" (42:5–6). The poetry of Job suggests that when we encounter God in nature, our sufferings fall into perspective before the vastness of creation and its immeasurable value. Not only God, but nature and goodness exceed Job's categories and expectations.

BIODIVERSITY AND PAUL'S IMAGE OF THE BODY OF CHRIST

Each year since 1996, a group of experts for the World Conservation Union has surveyed the world's plant and animal species, classifying in its Red List of Threatened Species those at risk of extinction and the reasons for their decline. When publishing their findings, the Union emphasizes how inextricably our lives and very survival are linked with biodiversity and its protection. In 2007 their list of the 18,306 species threatened with extinction included the critically endangered African Western gorilla and the Yangtze River dolphin.

Why should we as Christians care if species go extinct? Can we find a basis in our faith for such concern? Hearing one of Paul's epistles in light of our present context suggests an image to ground ecological vigilance. In his first letter to the Corinthians, Paul pleads for a unity that respects the variety of gifts given by the Spirit to members of the Christian community. He finds a creative metaphor for suggesting how the Corinthians are to understand their personal and social relationships in the new creation. Paul speaks of the body of Christ, but not as some abstract theory. Rather, this image is meant to expand and reorient Christian life, providing a template for addressing new situations. He turns to the example of the human body to illustrate his point: "The eye cannot say to the hand, 'I have no need of you,' nor again the head to the feet, 'I have no need of you'" (1 Cor 12:21).

In the centuries since Paul developed his body metaphor, our understanding of community has expanded dramatically. Today we find the Spirit's creative presence throughout the universe. Extending Paul's metaphor in light of these larger horizons, we might reflect on the value of all aspects of God's creation to the unity and diversity that as Christians we are to honor. This reading of Paul, which seems in keeping with the broader vision he suggests in his other letters, supports relationships of mutual care between humans and other species.

Reading Scripture is always an interpretive act when we apply it to our lives, and Paul's concern for the smallest member of the human body might be extended today to the situation a *New York Times* article bemoans: "Bugs Keep Planet Livable Yet Get No Respect." Although humans see themselves as the most indispensable aspect of creation, it is invertebrates like spiders, worms, and snails that keep the world moving along. Such species are crucial to the global ecosystem, and without them vertebrates like us could last only a few months. Scientists worry about the diminishment, and even extinction, of many invertebrate species. The loss is more fundamental than that of what we consider higher or more beautiful forms of life, such as orchids and blue herons. To paraphrase what Paul says of the smallest part of the human body, we cannot say to these invertebrates: "We have no need of you."

Spiritual practice keeps alive this respect for the intrinsic value of every creature. Gardening—long experienced as a space filled with solitude, contemplation, and creativity—is one of many areas where we can apply Paul's vision of a Spirit-enlivened body of creation. Birds, bees, and other animals have for millions of years scattered pollen and seed across the land, thus sustaining biodiversity. Now pesticides, narrowing habitats, and disease threaten our bee species. Along with the mysterious disappearance of honeybee colonies, there is concern that Franklin's bumblebee, once plentiful in northwestern California and southwestern Oregon, has gone extinct. We can offset some of this decline as we choose what to grow in our gardens and how to care for these plants. Protecting biodiversity as we garden means deciding what native plants are right for our area and removing invasive plants that threaten these species. Choosing plants that are highly drought tolerant and need little water helps to preserve this likewise threatened resource. In addition, certain plants that have been eliminated in the wild, for example, the blazing red Sprenger's tulip, still thrive in gardens and may not survive our century unless gardeners nurture them. When we embrace even the smallest of creatures with love, we join in the Spirit's work of sustaining the body of creation. Efforts to preserve biodiversity reflect the divine compassion that delights in and suffers with each individual. God knows each creature's inner form and essence as only an artist can perceive it. Jesus underscores this point when he insists that God cares about every single sparrow: "Are not five sparrows sold for two pennies? Yet not one of them is forgotten in God's sight" (Luke 12:6). His words are mainly about God's providence toward human beings: Fear should not keep us from living our faith, for we are held in God's safekeeping. But to make his point, Jesus uses as an analogy God's faithful care of sparrows—the cheapest of all the birds offered for sale. In doing so, he makes clear the worth each individual creature has in God's eyes.

ASKING NATURE TO TEACH US

What might Christian spirituality have in common with a renowned scientist whose specialty involves him in researching West Indies fire ant plagues? A great deal, it turns out. In *The Creation: An Appeal to Save Life on Earth*, Pulitzer Prize-winning biologist E. O. Wilson calls on people of faith to join biologists in an effort to stem pollution, global warming, and the Earth's rapidly declining biodiversity. His book takes the form of a letter to a Southern Baptist pastor. In it, he addresses the theme we have been exploring—how even the most humble species, those we might consider too inconspicuous to warrant our attention, are a masterpiece worth saving. Wilson gives this topic a different twist by pointing to the plight of the world's known species of amphibians, including frogs, toads, and salamanders, whose precipitous decline he finds alarming.

While he recognizes the fundamental differences between religion and science, Wilson suggests that the two might nonetheless offer each other mutual respect and unite in pursuit of common goals. Interestingly, one of the steps Wilson advocates is education. He notes that conservationists attribute the widespread indifference people feel for the living world to a failure in basic education in biology. The more we learn about other life forms and their immense diversity, Wilson argues, the more we will value them and, inevitably, ourselves as well.

Although Wilson is speaking from a scientific perspective, his proposal reminds us that reason as well as emotion, learning along with prayer belong to a holistic spirituality. Wilson's faith in the way full and accurate information develops empathy for all creatures was confirmed for me as I learned more about beavers. As part of my role as a creek steward (someone who takes responsibility for the maintenance of a section of our streams and creeks), I was invited to a workshop called, "Living with Beavers." In recent years coexisting with beavers in the Puget Sound area has required growing ingenuity as their population increases and they migrate to new locations. A beaver can dismantle a beautiful poplar in what seems like the blink of an eye and can fell more than two hundred trees a year. I still watch with some apprehension for signs that a beaver is constructing a lodge at my site along Thornton Creek, and plan ways to prevent damage to the trees that line its banks. But my sense of beavers changed dramatically after the conference, as I began to see the universe through their eyes. I learned that beavers are remarkable engineers who build impressive dams, canals, and lodges, carrying sticks, stones, and mud skillfully in their paws. They can see under water and, though slow on land, they are strong and graceful swimmers. Over time they help to maintain water levels, improve habitats for many forms of wildlife, and stabilize stream flow. Since the workshop I hold beavers in new esteem and see myself in a different kind of partnership with them.

Learning more about other species such as beavers will be easier with the launch of a three-hundred-million-page free encyclopedia on the Web. With a goal of describing all life on Earth, the *Encyclopedia of Life* will include what we know about 1.8 million species and will take about ten years to produce. Compiled by experts from leading scientific institutions and universities, the encyclopedia will also have clearly marked pages where amateurs can contribute their insights and sightings. Approached from the vantage point of faith, such an encyclopedia becomes a guide to contemplation, showing us the Divine revealed in a splendid and mysterious diversity across space and time.

Although both rest on accurate knowledge, the love of learning instilled by faith includes dimensions not found in the detached and objective observation that is the scientist's calling. The earlier chapters of the Book of Job recount an intense dialogue between Job and his friends around the traditional explanations they are offering for his immense suffering. In his rebuttal to their arguments, Job calls on the wisdom of other creatures as testimony to the truth that the very existence of every living being depends on God.

But ask the animals, and they will teach you;
the birds of the air, and they will tell you;
ask the plants of the earth, and they will teach you;
and the fish of the sea will declare to you.

(Job 12:7–8)

The rest of creation praises God and reveals divine wisdom by being who they are meant to be, by living according to God's intention in creating them.

Other biblical texts also indicate how nonhuman creatures embody wisdom about how to live faithfully. In the opening passage of the prophet Isaiah, we find God comparing human knowledge with the kind of knowing nonhuman creatures possess.

> The ox knows its owner,
> and the donkey its master's crib;
> but Israel does not know,
> my people do not understand. (1:3)

The prophet Jeremiah voices a similar divine complaint:

> Even the stork in the heavens knows its times;
> and the turtledove, swallow, and crane
> observe the time of their coming;
> but my people do not know
> the ordinance of the LORD. (8:7)

Scripture scholar Walter Brueggemann comments that the prophets' comparisons reveal how nonhuman creatures know the way each living thing relates to all others, how God's ordering of creation is meant to enhance all life. Asses and oxen recognize when it is time to be fed. Birds likewise know all that is necessary for them to know—the rhythm of the seasons, the times of seedtime and harvest, heat and cold of summer and winter. The awareness humans lack, according to these prophets, relates to the requirements and limits the Creator has instilled in the universe, to the elemental awareness that all creatures must adhere to the givens of creation. Though human beings know so much, they do not possess the knowledge that brings about peace rather than war, life rather than death.

We can, however, acquire the wise discernment that will enable us to change this, to take responsibility for the creaturely suffering that results from human activities. Wisdom comes not only through education and observation of the natural world but in the process of decision making in the family and the larger human community. Such decision making is always complex and complicated, since it requires balancing individual and communal needs, and human concerns with those of the nonhuman community.

Nature's ability to teach us becomes especially crucial today as we try to understand the impact of climate change on all living beings. Abundant evidence from around the globe, for instance, indicates that because of rising temperatures, crocuses, lilacs, and other flowering plants are blooming earlier each spring. The meaning of some changes remains unclear. Using a giant crane, University of Washington researchers have been able to rise 285 feet into old-growth Douglas fir trees. Looking down on their crowns, they have discovered that in 2007 they produced cones in abnormal quantities. Why they are doing this remains a mystery. What, these researchers wonder, are they telling us?

BRINGING IT TO PRAYER: PSALM 104

Many treatments of biodiversity sound an anxious and serious note today. Fear for the future of the Earth shrivels hearts and mutes joy. But in Psalm 104 we discover another way to raise awareness and gird constructive action. This biblical hymn invites us to join all creation in a song of unremitting praise for the diversity of our shared existence, to delight with God and other creatures at its vast beauty. In its closing lines, the psalm has harsh words for the wicked who shatter the world God has made, but in the rest of its imagery, the psalmist turns a grateful, at times playful, eye to God's gifts.

> In wisdom you have made them all;
> the earth is full of your creatures.
> Yonder is the sea, great and wide,
> creeping things innumerable are there,
> living things both small and great.
> There go the ships,
> and Leviathan that you formed to sport in it.
>
> (Ps 104:24–26)

God brings pattern and order out of the chaos. Like the first creation account in the Book of Genesis, the psalm pronounces creation, even the sea monster Leviathan, to be indeed very good. As in the Book of Job, all creatures have intrinsic value.

Nor does creation refer simply to a past event: "When you send forth your spirit, they are created; / and you renew the face of the ground" (v. 30). Creation and providence form a continuous reality; if the divine breath is withdrawn, death follows. If the Divine Face is hidden, all creation great and small gasps with dismay (vv. 29–30). God sustains each and every moment, sending springs to quench the thirst of wild animals, grass for the cattle, and plants for the people. The psalm is alive and throbbing with life, as nature finds its voice—winds serve as divine messengers, birds build nests and burst with song, the moon marks the seasons, young lions roar, and human beings fashion bread and wine. "These all look to you," the psalmist tells God—and content and secure within the embrace of an ongoing divine mercy, they lift up a cacophony of praise.

Moreover, we find in Psalm 104 an interdependent universe. No hierarchy or domination appears in the psalm. Rather it celebrates the intricate participation in God's work of every aspect of creation. In successive vignettes, the spotlight shines on each of the great and small creatures that make up the cosmos. They do not step forth as individual stars in a drama, however, but rather as distinctive voices in a complex chorus. None can make music alone. Fir trees provide nests for storks. The mountains furnish a suitable habitat for the wild goats and rock badgers. The darkness sets the stage for the emergence of the forest animals. People go about their work within an immense landscape teeming with activity (vv. 16–23).

How let this psalm renew our appreciation for the Earth community to which we belong and in which God rejoices? How hear this poem anew when repeated use often deadens the fresh immediacy of a psalm's language? Psalms figure prominently in many forms of communal prayer, and opening to their grace often means hearing their metaphors with new ears. Their very simplicity may help with that. The psalms have historically been an important part of the spiritual life due to the personal and immediate quality of their language. We recognize ourselves in them and find the words to name what we cannot otherwise quite identify—where we find ourselves within the whole range of human emotions. When we hear and sing the psalms we recognize our own deepest anger, longing, fear, gratitude, joy, and praise. These are ever changing, and reveal layers of the psalm's language that might not have reached us before.

Further, praying a psalm repeatedly can transform our hearts and minds at their deepest levels, gradually reshaping us according to God's Word. Because the psalms are poetry, they gradually instill in us certain modes of imagination. A traditional way of meditating on the psalms, one that accompanied the rise of monastic spirituality in the fourth century, is a good way to begin such prayer. It turns repetition into a positive, rather than negative, aspect of prayer by asking us to ruminate or meditate on the lines of a psalm, letting the words circulate within us. As with other poetry, learning the words by heart makes it easy to return to them often throughout the day. Several verses from Psalm 104 offer a helpful point of entry into such meditation.

> By the streams the birds of the air have their
> habitation....(v. 12)
> You have made the moon to mark the seasons....
> (v. 19a)
> I will sing praise to my God while I have being.
> (v. 33b)

Through this kind of prayer, the complexity and immensity of an interrelated universe is distilled into simple images that contain fundamental faith perspectives. Human beings exist within a wider cosmic community of life. Praise for creation's biodiversity commits us to its care and protection.

CHAPTER 4

THE DIVINE FACE
IN ALL FACES

But the relation to the face, always most intensely
focused in the interhuman, now demands of us planetary practices which find *face* across the width of the
world.

—Catherine Keller

🦋 In her book *Longing for Running Water*, the Brazilian theologian Ivone Gebara writes from a gritty awareness of the toll
that planetary destruction inflicts on the poor. Born in São
Paulo, Brazil, she says she has always lived in cities, and con-
fesses to having limited experience of plants, flowers, jungles,
seas, and similar aspects of nature. But Gebara's work with the
Brazilian poor women's movement roots her theology in neighborhoods without sewers and clean drinking water, in streets

strewn with garbage, and in the lives of children surrounded by rats, cockroaches, and mosquitoes. It is primarily from this perspective of a city life lacking access to green space and clean air and water, rather than from a mystical connection with nature, that Gebara advocates for a deeper communion between human beings and all other living beings. She warns that the green movement will not succeed unless it addresses the widespread suffering and urgent needs of all peoples. By showing that the destruction of the environment is linked to the poverty of her neighbors, Gebara makes clear how the two central issues of the twenty-first century—globalization and climate change—intersect with each other.

In a universe in which all living beings form one body, care of the Earth is inextricably bound up with work for peace and justice. We cannot claim to love God if we ignore our neighbor in need. Our love of nature rings hollow if we seek spiritual renewal in the wilderness or fight to protect trees from clear cutting but ignore injustices such as the dumping of toxic waste in vulnerable neighborhoods and impoverished countries. We share one life and draw from one divine Source. This calls for spiritual practice that is global in scope and grounded in universal compassion. Several streams of the tradition contribute to such a global, justice-oriented spirituality.

REVIVAL OF EMPHASIS
ON THE COMMON GOOD

The heart of the Catholic social tradition contains, in the rich concept of the common good, an invaluable guide for understanding global interdependence. Catholics in Alliance for the Common Good, a nonpartisan organization that partners with fifteen national Catholic social justice groups, summarizes this teaching in terms of four principles: (1) we are in this together; (2) preferential protection belongs to the most vulnerable in society; (3) the common good requires good governance; (4) principles supersede profit and power. These guidelines underscore the Christian vocation to influence the societies in which we live. Further, they extend beyond our faith communities, encouraging all citizens everywhere to take an active part in public life.

The biblical roots of the common good teaching lie in the Hebrew Scriptures, where we find the prophetic call to care for the widow, orphan, and stranger, and to create a just community that looks beyond its own needs to those of its most defenseless members: "Render true judgments, show kindness and mercy to one another; do not oppress the widow, the orphan, the alien, or the poor..." (Zech 7:8–10). Concern for the poor permeates the New Testament as well, and the call to love our neighbor as ourselves ties our well-being to that of the larger community. Only when we take care of one another will we find the freedom and security we seek.

Although the conviction that our lives are interdependent lies at the core of the common good tradition, this teaching cannot be reduced to a vague sense of compassion for the suffering of others. It requires recognition that we are, in fact, responsible for one another. Our well-being is thoroughly rooted in mutual care, and this means an ongoing commitment to the good of each individual. This kind of compassion directs us to provide for the welfare and dignity of all peoples, not just a few, and to a special focus on the poor and vulnerable. Further, the common good cannot be equated with charity, which is not a substitute for justice.

As it has become clear that the rapid deterioration of the environment threatens our collective future, the notion of the common good has been expanded to include the state of the biosphere. It may well be the determining issue, for the health of our planet's life support systems is inextricably tied to poverty, violence, war, and the hopes of all peoples for a good life. The depletion of forests and fisheries, water and food shortages—these all constitute fundamental threats to the common good.

In 2001, the United States Catholic bishops issued a pastoral letter linking the common good with climate change. The letter follows more than a decade of increasing attention to the environment on the part of the bishops and expresses particular concern for the impact of global warming on the world's poor. In their introduction to the pastoral, "Global Climate Change: A Plea for Dialogue, Prudence and the Common Good," the bishops situate climate change within a faith context and express concern for the planet as well as its people. Climate change, they believe, is not fundamentally a matter of economic and political theory or interest group pressure, but a question of faith: "It is about the future of God's creation and the one human family." How, they ask, can we learn to care for a creation that we are capable of altering, possibly irrevocably? And how can we protect creation and at the same time bring about justice and the common good? Their questions express the essential concerns of a global spirituality, one that asks us to find the divine face in the face of all living beings—even those who are strangers at the farthest reaches of the planet from us.

RECOGNIZING GOD IN THE STRANGER

On the first Earth Day in 1970, residents of cities across the United States gathered to advocate for tighter pollution controls. Citizens of Cleveland called for the cleanup of the Cuyahoga River, which was so contaminated by petroleum-based chemicals that its surface caught fire. People in smog-choked Los Angeles demanded cleaner air. Local issues dominated the discussion. During the ensuing decades, concern for ecological justice has become global, urgent, and focused on climate change, in terms of both the prevention of future temperature increases and adaptation to the consequences already in place.

According to the United Nations Intergovernmental Panel on Climate Change, the carbon dioxide that has already built up in the atmosphere means that as early as 2020, 75 million to 250 million people in Africa will experience water shortages, and the rivers and coastlines of Asia's large cities will be at high risk of flooding. Extensive areas will suffer species loss, and North Americans will face greater competition for water due to longer and hotter heat waves. Human suffering is therefore inevitable. But the poorest of the poor, in prosperous as well as less wealthy nations, will be hardest hit. If sea levels rise according to the projected models, impoverished residents of large coastal cities in the developing world will be the first to be flooded. Countries with inadequate health systems will find it hardest to cope with tropical diseases that spread because of warmer temperatures. Adapting to these consequences will require that we rise above private and national concerns to extend our compassion to species and people who are strangers to us.

Although migration is an ancient phenomenon, its size and shape today have redefined the meaning of homeland, borders, and strangers. Global warming is changing the migration patterns of numerous plant and animal species. Migrating birds such as sandpipers and kingfishers are arriving in Australia earlier and leaving later. Such changes in migration pose a serious threat to birds that fly longer distances, altering their life cycles, including when they reproduce, and putting them at risk for losing sources of food. Meanwhile the United Nations' 2002 International Migration Report estimates that there are roughly 175 million people migrating across the globe. The circumstances of many, including women as cheap labor, intertwine with globalization. Others are refugees from war, violence, and ethnic cleansing. They live in camps or as aliens in the countries to which they have fled, having left behind their land, home, and most of their belongings.

An ancient stream of spirituality teaches us to recognize God in these strangers. The Book of Genesis recounts how Sarah and Abraham, having abandoned family, friends, and homeland to pursue a divine call, have pitched their tent at Mamre in the hill country of Judah. In the oppressive heat of the day, three strangers arrive. Sarah and Abraham immediately bring them water, wash their feet, and prepare for them a tender calf, curds and milk, and cakes kneaded from choice flour. To Sarah's amazement, it is these strangers who proclaim God's promise that she will be released from her barrenness and blossom like spring, will give birth to a child in the face of despair (18:1–15). Fruitfulness and redemption spring from hospitality and generosity.

This theme of the invisible face of God shifts its shape as we proceed from Genesis through the rest of Scripture. In *The Hidden Face of God*, Richard Elliott Friedman probes God's mysterious disappearance in the course of the Bible. Friedman discovers a gradual movement from a world where God is known in manifest ways to one in which God's face is increasingly hidden: "In Genesis and Exodus you see Him; by Ezra and Esther you don't." The Hebrew Bible, Friedman notes, uses the metaphorical phrase, "God hides his face," more than thirty times. In the later books of the Hebrew Bible, God sometimes speaks through inspired leaders and prophets, but there is less direct divine communication and there are fewer miracles. Perhaps, Friedman suggests, this concealing of the Divine points to the responsibility we human beings are to assume for our universe.

The counsel to find God's face hidden in the strangers in our midst occurs throughout the New Testament as well. In the parable of the last judgment, those who extend mercy to the hungry, thirsty, naked, sick, or imprisoned are amazed to learn that in serving the least valued members of society they were in fact encountering the Divine: "Truly I tell you, just as you did it to one of the least of these who are members of my family, you did it to me." And those who failed to respond with compassion to others in need are equally astonished to realize that they had missed a meeting with God (Matt 25:31–46).

What if we were to use Jesus' parable of the last judgment as a lens through which to view the entire cosmos and the diverse beings that inhabit it? How would we be changed if we imaginatively entered and prayed this parable from a global perspective? Within such an expanded context, Jesus' injunction turns our attention to suffering across the planet. Feeding the hungry, clothing the naked, and tending to the sick and imprisoned require that we protect the native habitats of plants and animals, develop farming methods that preserve natural resources and energy reserves, and clean up our polluted oceans and rivers. In such prayer we allow Jesus' parable to transform us. It prepares us to notice the stranger who appears as the homeless and hungry in our neighborhoods, but it also illumines the larger political and economic realities that affect the most vulnerable beings in the universe and makes clear our responsibility to address these inequities.

Service to Christ in the neighbor was a driving passion of the fourteenth-century reformer and doctor of the Church, Catherine of Siena. In her mystical conversations with God she learned a new twist on the importance of charity and on the role that the otherness of our neighbor plays in shaping community. Catherine lived and wrote against the backdrop of devastation caused by the black death and the mercenary armies that engaged in constant warfare on behalf of their cities. Adding to the chaos, the papacy had fled the dangers of Rome to a palace in Avignon, France. In the midst of these historical circumstances, she worked for peace and reconciliation on both the local and wider stage, seeking to carry out Jesus' directive to her: "The service you cannot do to me you must render your neighbors."

Catherine discovered that dealing with the otherness we find in our midst lies at the heart of what it means to be the Body of Christ. In the *Dialogue*, a work in which she discusses the spiritual life through a series of colloquies, God tells her that in this life we are bound to our neighbors by the chain of charity, whether we want it or not. Even if we do not desire to live in love for our neighbors, we are still held by the force of these bonds: "That you may practice charity in action and in will, I in my providence did not give to any one person or to each individually the knowledge for doing everything necessary in human life." Although we might lose our will for charity, we would still be forced by our needs to practice it in action.

In our century we might express Catherine's mystical insight by acknowledging that no nation by itself can protect its people against threats such as global warming. Addressing them requires that all the diverse gifts available to the global community be used on behalf of our neighbors, near and far.

ROOTING OUR COMPASSION IN THE HEART OF GOD

Widening the poles of our compassion tent may alarm rather than reassure us. Often the suffering of immediate friends and family members—work problems and financial struggles, accidents and medical emergencies, marriage conflicts and mental illness—depletes our energy reserves. The afflictions of others prove too much to bear, along with our own, and we turn away out of a certain kind of self-protection. If tragedy strikes, the initial instinct is to protect those we know best. When reports of climate change surface, we may calculate its impact on our region rather than advert to its consequences for countries that have contributed least to global warming, such as Bangladesh, which is threatened first by floods from melting Himalayan glaciers and then by drought as glacier-fed rivers dry up.

The first Christian disciples experienced this same depletion of their capacity to care. As Jesus enters the Garden of Gethsemane, he asks his disciples to watch and pray with him, telling them: "I am deeply grieved, even to death; remain here, and keep awake" (Mark 14:34). Distressed and agitated, Jesus pours out his lament to God, returning to his disciples several times only to find them sleeping. Like us, these disciples discover that good intentions are sometimes hard to sustain; flesh is weaker than spirit. Numbness and sleep overtake them in the face of impending dangers. The same is often true of us, which is why sustaining compassion over the long haul requires participation in God's own compassion for the world.

Through prayer we root our compassion in the heart of God; that enables us to love others with an all-encompassing embrace. When a Sufi friend wrote Thomas Merton to ask how he prayed, Merton replied that his method of meditation was centered on the presence and love of God. It was not, however, an effort to think about anything; rather, it was a kind of praise rising out of nothingness and silence. Finally, he wrote, prayer is a "seeking of the Face of the Invisible." But Merton believed that such contemplation unites us with our brothers and sisters and all other beings in the universe. We find them in God. In *New Seeds of Contemplation*, Merton describes the nature of the care and communion that flow from Christian prayer: "When you and I become what we are really meant to be, we will discover not only that we love one another perfectly but that we are both living in Christ and Christ in us and we are all one Christ. We will see that it is he who loves in us." When compassion flows from contemplation, its roots lie deep in God, and it is the divine

Spirit who sustains us. Without that Spirit, we run the risk of going dry, no longer capable of generosity, kindness, or love.

As Merton reminds us, through prayer we gradually come to love with the very love of God. John of the Cross underscores this point when he speaks of contemplation as "a secret, peaceful and loving inflow of God, which, if not hampered, fires the soul in the spirit of love." In prayer we open up our hearts as a space that God increasingly fills. Then when we are asked to respond to tragedy, we find that God is already there, that God weeps with the universe's pain and longs for the redemption of all creation that we ourselves desire: "For a long time I have held my peace, / I have kept still and restrained myself; / now I will cry out like a woman in labor, / I will gasp and pant" (Isa 42:14).

Through prayer, we become partners with a God in hard labor to birth justice and a new heaven and earth. This God urges us beyond violence and exploitation to ever greater inclusiveness and reconciliation with all beings. Left to our own efforts, we despair of such a vision ever becoming a reality. But we do not depend solely on our own limited resources to heal the world's brokenness; we do our part and then rely on God for the rest.

MAKING THE CONNECTIONS: PRACTICES FOR A GLOBAL SPIRITUALITY

Like hazy breath on a cold day, the term *globalization* often enters conversation without clear definition. This may be due to the mixed content and consequences it encompasses, realities as diverse as financial markets and interreligious dialogue. Consider, for a moment, the dense and intricate web of connections that weaves across our planet: technology links peace movements and personal blogs from every continent, bugs hitchhike on freighters from distant ports, art and ideas cross borders, word of an individual's triumph or tragedy arrives instantaneously in other cities across the world. Many of these exchanges enhance human community. But globalization holds both promise and peril. From an ecological and justice perspective, it is its darker veins that most urgently need to be exposed and addressed. During the decades since World War II, rapid economic exchange has impoverished peoples and destroyed the environment around the globe. Individuals and corporations from wealthier nations have invested in Asia, Africa, and South America, extracting profits without concern for the well-being of the countries or the Earth. The gap between the rich and poor has widened, and many indigenous cultures have been marginalized.

Across the world the exploitation of natural resources by transnational oil, mining, and timber companies has contaminated the land and polluted the water. Latin American peoples from Chile to Mexico are fighting these destructive intrusions of globalization, struggling, often in the face of threats and violence, to preserve their resources from foreign exploitation. As part of this growing "liberation ecology" movement, Catholic communities in Honduras and Guatemala have united to protect their land, water, and timber from local and North American corporations. They see their action—battling foreign-owned gold mines that deplete the water tables and dry up wells, or logging that strips away resources to nourish the prosperity of others—as God's work on behalf of their people.

Many organizations now offer opportunities for others throughout the world to take an active part in these countries' struggle to preserve their landscapes and resources. But practices for a global spirituality also start right where we are, in the midst of our everyday prayer and decisions. These deepen our awareness of our connections with others across the planet and of the impact they feel from our decisions. Such meditation helps to change our understanding and values and then takes us where we need to go next in helping to heal the dark strands of our planetary web.

CLOTHING OUR WORLD

Since globalization often separates us from the impact of our actions, it is important that we learn how our choices of energy, food, transportation, and clothing affect other people and God's creation. An ordinary object can awaken us to global connections that may now be invisible. As we become better informed and take that information to prayer, grace often leads us to further action.

Draw a circle on a piece of paper, your computer, or your cell phone. Then begin a meditation on the positive or negative threads that tie the clothing you wear to people and places around the globe.

Choose a piece of your wardrobe—a jacket, sweater, blouse, running shoes—and write it in the circle. During the course of the next days or weeks, weave into the circle as much information as you can gather about this object. Where was it made, for example, in China, Vietnam, or India? What are the conditions in the garment factory it came from? What material or materials are found in it, for example, cotton, hemp, wool? How does the use of these fibers affect workers and the Earth?

If you got a great price when you bought it, did this effort to pay as little as possible add to exploitation and pollution in the country where it was made? For example, if the clothing came from China, are that country's pollution problems tied to your low price? Would you be willing to pay more to improve those conditions?

Did you have other choices for finding the garment you needed—a thrift store, a clothing exchange with friends, making it yourself? What will become of the piece of clothing when you no longer want to wear it? The purpose of this meditation is to raise awareness and then let God's grace work in you as you ponder what you discover. It can take a shorter form with any object you enjoy, for example, learning whether your chocolate or coffee are fair trade, and what that means for the farmers who produce them.

Meditation slows us down enough to reflect on how consumer goods are woven from the lives of those who labor in garment factories around the globe. It alerts us to the cost to the Earth of obtaining the lowest possible prices. We learn how conventional farming for cotton harms the air, water, soil, and farmer, and how the rush to meet manufacturing quotas creates dangerous working conditions for others who are mothers and fathers, sisters and brothers, sons and daughters like us.

BREATHING AS A PATH TO DEEPER AWARENESS OF THE GLOBAL COMMUNITY

Attention to the breath is a part of prayer in many traditions. It can also increase our awareness of the way we are bonded with plants, animals, inorganic substances, and peoples of all races, religions, and cultures.

Begin by placing yourself in a comfortable position and become aware that you are in God's presence. Your eyes can be open or closed.

Then notice your breath. Do not try to change or deepen it. Simply stay with this awareness for some moments.

Realize that the Spirit of God keeps you alive, and give thanks for this gift.

As you continue to breathe, become aware that every breath you take carries molecules that have lived in the lungs of all the human beings that have ever lived.

Then recall that all creatures everywhere breathe this same air. What diminishes them diminishes you. You might make this concrete by naming regions of the globe: Antarctica, Siberia, Spain, Peru.

As you continue to breathe, let some biblical images move through you to deepen the ancestry of your breath.

In the second creation story (Gen 2:7), God breathes into the first humans the breath of life and they become living beings.

The animals that enter Noah's ark are "two and two of all flesh in which there was the breath of life" (Gen 7:15, 6:17).

Psalm 104 says of all living beings: "...when you take away their breath, they die and return to their dust. / When you send forth your spirit, they are created..." (29b–30a).

Return to your breathing and rest for some moments in the web of creation that is vivified by God's Spirit. Let this wider sense of your breath stay with you during your other activities of the day.

EXPANDING OUR IMAGES OF GOD

Greater ties with other peoples enable us to find the Divine Face in faces around the planet, thus enlarging our image of God. Genesis is our guide here, in its message that every person—male and female—is created in God's image. A greater range of divine images opens a wider sphere of human possibilities for all people and supports their dignity and equality. If we keep alive a diverse store of images, they enrich and qualify one another, pointing through their interaction to the transcendence of God.

This contemplation can be done in the midst of work or another activity as you take in the different faces of those around you, or you can gather some of these images and sit with them during times of prayer.

Look on these many-hued and diverse faces coming to you from around the globe—suffering, tortured, buoyed, jubilant, angry, strong—and see what images of God they suggest to you. Encounters with other human beings multiply now in every form of travel and media. What can these faces teach us about our multifaceted God? What can we know of God if we move beyond our familiar images to include these many faces?

Name a divine image that comes to you and let your prayer flow from it. An image or metaphor is like a lens through which we catch a glimpse of God. Then take one of these unfamiliar images with you to view the world through its lens during the day.

You might close with an image of the face of God, kindly and favorable, revealed in a prayer from the Samburu of East Africa.

My God, guard us
in the narrow and deep valleys full of dangers,
and in the plains without end,
and in the fords we cross small or large.
And God said, "All right!"

FOCUSING THE IGNATIAN DAILY EXAMEN ON GLOBAL CONCERNS

Ignatian spirituality contains a practice helpful for broadening our awareness to include global concerns. The *awareness examen* or examination of consciousness requires finding some moments for quiet reflection during the day or at bedtime. This allows God's grace to illumine what has been happening and to help us notice undercurrents we may have sensed but not brought into full awareness.

In the *Spiritual Exercises*, Ignatius describes five aspects of the examen. We begin with a prayer of gratitude for the day's blessings, naming some in detail. Then we ask the Spirit to give us the insight and freedom to look honestly at our motives and actions, and not let us hide behind deception and excuses. At the end we may ask for courage or forgiveness.

Those who practice the examen often concentrate on inner movements or the dynamics of human relationships. A simple question or two can form the heart of a more global focus: When was I most aware of the impact of my actions on other creatures throughout the planet? When was I least aware?

The examen offers a structured way to integrate our inner work with concern for the larger environment in which we live, broadening our spirituality to include the entire planet. Like the other spiritual practices suggested here, it can show us how our personal struggles are deeply connected to the polluted air we breathe, the push for more consumer goods, and the violence that surrounds us in society.

CHAPTER 5

WHERE WONDER
LEADS US

But I believe that the more clearly we can focus our
attention on the wonders and realities of the world
around us, the less taste we shall have for destruction.

—Rachel Carson

In the summer of 2006 doctors diagnosed my brother with
multiple myeloma, an aggressive and incurable blood cancer. He
immediately began a regimen of anticancer drugs and later
decided to undergo a stem-cell transplant. Since his own stem
cells, not those of a donor, would be used for the procedure, the
initial stage of treatment focused on harvesting these cells. On a
late January morning, as he and his wife prepared to leave for the
Seattle Cancer Care Alliance, they were amazed to see outside
their kitchen window a row of purple crocuses fully in bloom.

The flowers seemed a miracle, defying the season. Was their early blooming perhaps a harbinger of hope?

Later that spring, after enduring weeks of chemotherapy, hair loss, nausea, and fatigue, my brother learned that the transplant had failed. As he struggled to absorb this devastating news, the garden he had nurtured over the years continued to offer its beauty in an exchange of grace with him. Cherry trees blossomed, lilacs and rhododendrons flowered, and roses filled the yard with their fragrance. Unable now to tend them because his cancer treatments had so weakened his immune system, he watched in wonder as each returned the care he had bestowed on it.

Spirituality begins in wonder. To understand something of what happens to us in wonder or awe, we can turn back in history to the thinking of the nineteenth-century theologian John Henry Newman. Newman described two different ways of assenting to the existence of a personal and present God. One path takes us through an intellectual exercise by way of proof and analysis; God is known in the assent to a proposition. Along the other path, which Newman called *real assent*, we encounter God as the object of devotion, a religious reality. Wonder is such a religious experience.

Although most of us can recall moments of wonder, we might not fully realize just how significant a role it plays in shaping our values and actions. Nor do we always think of it as an emotion. Wonder receives less attention than emotions such as anger, fear, and sadness, but it is even more essential to our care of the Earth and to our personal and communal survival. The gift of wonder expands awareness, connecting us to the wider universe and fostering empathy and compassion. When we are weary of terrors—nuclear threats, violence, dangers to the planet—wonder suggests a transcendent dimension to existence, a something *more* present within the material world that sustains our joy and courage. In the midst of awe, we are moved to ask about the meaning of existence itself, to ponder the cause and purpose of unexpected moments of beauty and grace, and to respond with gratitude. Neglected aspects of life suddenly shift into perspective. In these and other ways, wonder sustains long-term action on behalf of Earth.

WONDER LEADS TO EMPATHY AND COMPASSION

Many fields of study—moral philosophy, neuroscience, holistic spirituality—are taking a renewed interest in emotions such as wonder today. Their findings indicate that emotions are much more central to human action than previously realized. Not only do they mobilize us to act, but they redirect our attention, information, energy, and goals. Think of a time you felt a sense of wonder, how the sight of a hummingbird hovering outside your window steadied your gaze, lifted your spirits, and firmed your resolve. Being held in wonder, anger, or fear constitutes a continuous state of the whole person, an ongoing activity during which we are continually evaluating new information and allowing it to influence us. Any attempt to live the Christian faith must fully incorporate emotional experience.

The emotion of fear initially promises to be an especially effective motive for addressing threatening events such as species extinction or climate change. It alerts us to danger and propels us to action. Many scientific studies about the state of the planet kindle fear. In *Field Notes from a Catastrophe*, Elizabeth Kolbert recounts her conversations with scientific experts and those affected by climate disruption in places such as Alaska, Greenland, and Oregon. In each location, Kolbert heard similar expressions of present loss and fear for future generations. "The world is going too fast," says an Inuit hunter from Banks Island in the Northwest Territories in Canada. In recent years he and his neighbors had started seeing robins, birds they had no name for, birds drawn to the Territories by warmer weather. This warming trend initially seemed like a positive thing, he tells Kolbert, until it began to erode their traditional way of life, including their hunting. "Our children may not have a future," concludes the hunter. "I mean, all you people, put it that way. It's not just happening in the Arctic. It's going to happen all over the world." Kolbert herself does not believe we can be counted on to do the right thing. "It may seem impossible to imagine that a technologically advanced society could choose, in essence, to destroy itself," she says, "but that is what we are now in the process of doing."

Studies such as Kolbert's can motivate us to take action. Fear's first instinct, however, is to defend the self, so it tends to produce a narrow vision and a self-protective response. Communal boundaries tighten and the instinct rises to defend one's territory. We lock doors, build fences, and establish gated communities. Nations put their own interests first. Rather than looking for more equitable ways to share the planet's limited resources, under the influence of fear countries resort to rhetoric and the stockpiling of weapons.

When isolated from the other emotions, fear restricts our field of vision, whereas wonder expands it. One of the few emotions that moves us toward openness and connection, wonder takes us closer to our environment. It pulls us out of ourselves as we reach toward the source of life or beauty. Sometimes children express this by literally lifting their hands or reaching their arms spontaneously toward a sunrise or a peacock. They throw back their heads in laughter and chase after what delights them. The ethical theorist Martha Nussbaum declares that no other emotion matches wonder's ability to increase empathy and compassion. She believes that wonder most clearly enables human beings to move beyond self-interest in order to recognize and respond to others on their own terms. Freed from the prison of private preoccupations, we embrace all of creation. Though an experience of wonder may last only a few moments, it influences us for a lifetime.

Wonder suspends our usual goal-oriented activity and our tendency to break things down into manageable size. This distinguishes it from other emotions, such as fear and anger, which tend to move us toward immediate action. In wonder we have a particularly strong sense of the present and its fullness. We come to appreciate the value of both persons and nature, and this provides a foundation for subsequent action.

Often an appreciation of the grandeur of the cosmos elicits not only awe, but restraint. How does this happen? When we experience wonder, we are most fully aware of the value of what we encounter—a full moon resplendent in a dark winter sky, an ancient oak tree draped with Spanish moss, a little girl turning cartwheels in a city playground—and less intent on how these realities might meet our own needs or plans. At that moment we are not thinking of how the moon might be an apt object for exploration, how the oak tree would make a nice desk for our study, or how the girl could teach us cartwheels. Wonder pulls us out of ourselves and takes us to the contemplation of living beings rather than to the planning of action toward them. We are responding to the tug of another creature in all its amazing complexity. This relationship, not the usefulness of an object, becomes the focus of our interest.

In human life as well as nature, where we fix our attention affects our perceptions and actions. In his photographic essay, *Another Africa*, Robert Lyons asks us to focus for a moment on Africa's unimaginable beauty rather than on the negative images usually conveyed to us. During his extensive travels throughout Kenya, Ethiopia, Senegal, Ghana, and other parts of Africa, Lyons lets his camera convey the untapped strength found in scenes from daily life. What he hopes to show us is what we share as beings in the universe, our commonality rather than the differences that divide us.

Wonder's expansive and unifying power makes possible true mutuality with a wider circle of beings. It redefines the boundaries of our concern in a way that enlarges reverence. Think, for example, of the oceans. They cover 70 percent of the Earth's surface. Not surprising then that the psalmist frequently cries out in amazement at the spectacle of billowing waves and so vast an array of sea creatures: "Yonder is the sea, great and wide, / creeping things innumerable are there, / living things both small and great" (Ps 104:25). Learning more about the mysteries of the sea only deepens awe. Even in the complete darkness of their deepest recesses, colorful sea creatures exist in designs beyond our imagining. Amid toxic plumes, there lives a more dense population of life than anywhere on Earth. The Creator of the seas appears as an artist of immense imagination and largesse.

WONDER EMBRACES CREATION'S COMPLEXITY

Even when caught up in wonder, we cannot ignore the mystery of suffering in creation. If anything, the question of evil intensifies as we notice fragile blossoms buffeted by the wind and learn of viruses that cause illnesses such as AIDS and dengue fever. An old Buddhist tale tells of two monks who stand on top of a mountain and survey all of nature. "How horrible!" says one, tears welling up in his eyes. "They are eating each other." "Don't be so upset," the other says to him. "Really, they are feeding each other." Each monk names a partial truth.

Emotions are not one single thing—simply anger, fear, sadness, or wonder. Rather, like light, they exist on a spectrum composed of many colors. This complexity means that wonder often arrives mixed with other feelings such as fear and sadness. We know that the nature whose beauty we admire can unleash killer earthquakes, hurricanes, and floods. This wild power feeds our sense of awe, but it also gives rise to the conviction that we must control and master nature. Denise Levertov captures this ambivalence toward creation beautifully in her poem "Threat." She writes of the way you can feel blessed to live for years with a large pine tree for a neighbor, not minding the needles that fall on your flowers or the cones that drop on your deck. Only during a Northwest windstorm do you become aware that underneath this appreciation of the tree's beauty there lies the fear that some day it might come crashing "down on your house, on you in your bed." After a particularly damaging wind storm in 2006, Seattleites began to see the trees they loved as now menacing and eyed them warily. Letters to the local newspaper spoke of the "revenge of the trees."

The realm of the Divine is both glorious and fearful. In the revelation at Mount Sinai, Yahweh descends on the mountain in fire and speaks to the thousands of Israelites gathered below. The divine fire and voice terrify them (Exod 19:11–22). When the divine messenger approaches Mary of Nazareth, she is first told not to be afraid. We become uneasy when God draws close. The Bible describes religious awe as an experience of God's transcendence, an attitude captured by the phrase, *the fear of the Lord*. A gift of the Spirit, it implies deep reverence for the Divine and marks the beginning of wisdom (Prov 1:7). Both the gentle and the wild qualities of nature evoke awe before God's creation. The biblical depiction of nature embraces her renewal and beauty, but also her chaos and unpredictability, and the deaths that precede new life.

Much of nature's current suffering stems from human action. Consider the oceans. My childhood visits to the sea brought a peace I could not find far from its shores. I traveled to

the Oregon coast to take in patches of light dancing like dia-
monds on the waves of the Pacific Ocean, and starfish clinging
to jagged rocks. But in recent years my contemplation has taken
a different turn. I cannot ignore the oil-soaked seagulls washed
lifeless onto the sand after a spill, or the seaweed twisted with
empty Coke cans and plastic bags. Creation seems tarnished. In
"God's Grandeur," the poet Gerard Manley Hopkins not only
marvels at the divine beauty present in creation, he laments that
it is so "bleared, smeared with toil."

A walk on the beach, no longer an unalloyed experience of
divine artistry, takes me now to empathy for the waters I have
viewed primarily as a refuge for so many decades. This empathy
forms the foundation for work on behalf of urban creeks as well
as ocean beaches. In the Puget Sound there are several projects to
"daylight" streams, a strange expression in one way, but also a
parable for what needs to happen on behalf of nature. In the case
of these streams, concrete highways or shopping mall parking
lots have buried them underground. Bringing them back into the
light allows them to flow freely, thereby providing a chance that
fish will return to their waters and that people and plants will
line their banks as they flow to the sea.

If we stay with experiences of wonder, they take us to ever
broader vistas. Grace prods us to praise the majesty of the sea,
but also to heal the twisted remains of human carelessness. Now
we must deal with anger and fear as well as with peace and
beauty. We are not alone in this, however, for we are accompanied by the Wisdom we meet in these moments of awe.

ATTENTION READIES US FOR WONDER

In both his person and his teaching Jesus renews our sense
of mystery about the meaning of existence. The gospels tell us

that those who followed him encountered the unexpected and were amazed. Their hearts and minds were opened and they left with new energy. In the gospels, such amazement expresses the crowds' admiration and surprise at Jesus: "And they were filled with great awe and said to one another, 'Who then is this, that even the wind and the sea obey him?'" (Mark 4:41). People began to follow Jesus, but their amazement was just the first step on the journey. The capacity to be amazed and to wonder is a gift of the Spirit who gradually enables Jesus' disciples to proclaim the marvels of God.

We cannot manufacture wonder. However, though it comes as a gift, we can prepare for its arrival. We do this by paying attention, a disposition of heart and mind basic to all prayer. In *Waiting for God*, the French philosopher and mystic Simone Weil states the equation between prayer and attention in a radical way: "Prayer consists of attention. It is the orientation of all the attention of which the soul is capable toward God." If we turn to the gospels, we see not only how Jesus challenged his disciples to be alert and ready for God's coming (Matt 25:1–13), we also find evidence of how closely Jesus noticed the wonders of nature. His teaching brims with analogies that reveal a lifetime of attending to its mysteries. The gospels portray Jesus as a teacher who had really watched the sparrow, carefully studied seeds scattered randomly, looked closely at a mustard seed and a dying fig tree, observed the way the wind blows where it will. He turned to nature to teach his disciples how to read the signs of the times. If they can tell by the clouds rising in the west that rain is on its way, or know that when the wind blows from the south, it will be hot, why can they not interpret the present time (Luke 12:54–56)? Jesus not only pointed to aspects of the natural world to fill his stories and teaching, he taught us how to view nature—as a revelation of God's ways.

More and more people make their way in the world while plugged into iPods or cell phones. This allows for only a vague awareness of our immediate surroundings and puts us at risk for missing moments of wonder. The senses of smell, touch, taste, and vision are neutralized by this concentration on hearing. In contrast, a lifetime of paying attention and truly seeing what is all around us comes through in an unlikely source. Although she could neither see nor hear, Helen Keller had so finely tuned her other senses that upon entering a greenhouse she could tell the names of flowers by their smell alone. Touching the lips of her friend Mark Twain, she followed his colorful stories of life on the Mississippi. Keller's writings are filled with the aromas and tastes of life, and they stir in us an appreciation for what it might mean to fill up our senses.

At its root, attention means to stretch toward something; when we pay attention to anything, we open out to it. The marine biologist Rachel Carson remarks in her ground-breaking book on ecology, *Silent Spring*, that most of us walk through the world unaware of its beauties and wonders and the "strange and terrible intensity of the lives that are being lived about us." But even a small taste of the wonders of the Earth increases our appetite for learning more. Carson believed that moral actions flow from identification and empathy; her goal therefore was not simply to give us knowledge about nature but to teach us how to *feel* about it. When we take action, such as avoiding the use of the synthetic pesticides whose dangers she exposed, we do so out of appreciation for creation, not from fear of reprisals.

As Carson entered midlife, her niece died, and she suddenly faced the responsibility of raising her grandnephew, Roger. While grappling with this new challenge, she wrote an article for *Woman's Home Companion* entitled "Help Your Child to Wonder." Later published with photographic illustrations as *A Sense of Wonder*, it captures her vision of how best to help each new generation develop a reverence for life. Carson was convinced that our most important gift to children is the cultivation of a sense of wonder that will last them a lifetime. She believed wonder keeps us close to the sources of strength and protects us from what she termed the boredom and disenchantment of the later years.

PRIMARY WONDER AND THE GIFT OF EXISTENCE

The essayist Ben Birnbaum tells how once when he visited his mother, he found her sitting in the front room of their Brooklyn home, gazing out at the mature London plane trees lining the neighborhood streets. "Did you know," his mother said to him, "that leaves have tiny holes on the bottom for drinking water? And when it's about to rain, they know it and they turn themselves over. How can anybody believe there is no God?"

When we experience wonder, it leads to the question of final causality: How can this be? Bird migration offers an example. We have not yet solved the mystery of how a tiny bobolink can make its way across oceans and continents, safely following a course from Maine to Argentina and back every year. Or how to explain the artistic intricacy of the world's coral reefs. Though they occupy only one-tenth of 1 percent of the earth's surface, they contain as many as nine million species.

But even if we feel no sense of wonder when we see the exploding mauve, red, and orange of a sunset or hear the song of a whip-poor-will in the summer marshes, we find ourselves marveling at times simply at the bare fact that we are alive, that any created world exists at all. This kind of awe might be summed up in attempts to answer the perennial question, "Why is there something rather than nothing?" Moment by moment all created beings are lured out of chaos into existence. At each instant life emerges from all the deaths around us. Paul speaks of the God who raised Jesus from the dead as the God "who gives life to the dead and calls into existence the things that do not exist" (Rom 4:17).

The poet Denise Levertov calls this realization that our very existence depends on God's sustaining power, *primary wonder.* We know this creative presence as the quiet background to each day's activities, the horizon that moves with us into each of life's stages. But once in a while—perhaps when we are spared a dire diagnosis or a fatal accident—our ordinary ways of experiencing the world are suspended and we recognize who and where we are in the most fundamental sense.

Though it is often extinguished by daily distractions, spiritual practices can teach us to nurture primary wonder. In his *Spiritual Exercises*, Ignatius of Loyola asks us to meditate on what it means to be a creature. A fundamental moment of the *Exercises* comes in the acceptance and celebration of our creaturehood. This experience of being amazed is for Ignatius a graced self-transcendence. In his spiritual diary he calls it *affectionate awe*, and it characterizes his attitude toward God.

Recognition that we need not have been given life pervades many of the psalms. The psalmist proclaims that God creates the world, not in some distant past, but at every moment. God sustains all things or they would not exist.

When you send forth your spirit, they are created;
and you renew the face of the ground.

(Ps 104:30)

Raising this question of why there is anything at all connects us more deeply to the universe. We cease taking it for granted. We feel more alive and attentive to all that surrounds us.

WONDER AS A WAY TO GRATITUDE

In our consumer society, marketers convince us not only that we need something more, but that this more should be something *else*, something other than what we already possess—a different car, the latest soda, a house in a better neighborhood. In contrast, wonder gives rise to gratitude, to an appreciation of the gifts that already mark our existence. Spiritual practices that nurture appreciation provide a potent antidote to the drive to accumulate that so threatens our planet. Gratitude teaches us to want less, simplify our lives, and care for what we have been given.

When we cease to take for granted the small and large wonders that permeate our existence, thanksgiving and praise arise as natural responses to the God who scatters gifts so freely about. Our hearts overflow. Practicing gratitude begins at the same point as wonder, with attention to the blessings that surround us and the realization that we have not earned them. These wonders need not be as grand and majestic as snow-capped mountain peaks. They can be as small, yet as amazing, as a child's first step. Then when we sense a restless yearning or the urge to reach for more things, we learn to gently return our attention to what we already have at hand: the powers of sight and hearing, the breeze gently moving through the trees, coffee and cereal before us on the breakfast table. Any number of practices allow gratitude to gradually become our characteristic way of being in the world— starting meals with a grace that makes gratitude intentional, deepening our understanding of the Eucharist as a thanksgiving supper, closing our day with a litany of small or large gifts. Phrases from the psalms carry the theme throughout the day: "How good it is to sing praises to our God" (147:1); "I give you thanks, O LORD, with my whole heart" (138:1). Daily blessings—for waking and sleeping, recovery from illness or strength for a journey—also provide occasions for wonder and gratitude.

The twentieth-century Jewish rabbi, teacher, and prophet Abraham Joshua Heschel instilled the importance of radical amazement in many Christians as well as Jews. Although he died in 1972, before the ecological movement reached its present prominence, Heschel inspired people of many faiths with his vision of the centrality of wonder and its relationship to gratitude, prayer, and social activism. Heschel believed that religion arises as a fundamental response to wonder, and that the chief characteristic of the religious person's attitude toward history and nature is radical amazement.

Born in Warsaw in 1907, Heschel fled the city just before the Nazi invasion in 1939. He eventually made it to America, where he spent the rest of his life teaching in Jewish and Christian seminaries. He contributed in major ways to the most challenging issues of our time: interfaith dialogue and cooperation, peace, and social justice. An official observer at the Second Vatican Council, he influenced its statement on the church's relationship with Judaism. He took a prophetic stand against the Vietnam War and marched in the cause of civil rights alongside his close friend Martin Luther King, Jr.

Heschel loved nature, and his writing reveals an appreciation of the planet's grandeur. He also sensed that something was very wrong with the way human beings were living. He feared that a sense of wonder almost inevitably declines with the advance of civilization, and he considered this "an alarming symptom of our state of mind." He was convinced that humankind "will not perish for want of information; but only for want of appreciation." Heschel's witness continues to inspire a sense of responsibility for our troubled world, and an appreciation of prayer as a way of coming to need what God needs and to feel what God feels. True to his Hasidic roots, he never lost sight of the mystery that encompasses us and of prayer as an act of empathy and hope through which we can discover our joyous place in God's cosmos.

Before Heschel, another Jewish rabbi taught us how the meaning of wonder illumines an additional aspect of global tragedy: How can we feel gratitude for the goodness of our lives when others are enduring such crushing losses? How can we reconcile our small daily joys with the sorrows of the world? Jesus showed us how to give thanks, even in troubled times, for the beauty of flower and field, the comfort of food and friends, and the ever present mercy of God. He squarely faced the evils in our universe, but he taught us to celebrate the light wherever it appears, so that it might expand to illumine a darkened world. Jesus' death and resurrection were the fullest expressions of this paradox, but it is contained also in stories of the last who are first, the emptiness that is fullness, and the lost who are found.

Translated into the realm of "worldsorrow," this means that as we make our way through troubling events we will indeed know fear and grief. But there is room also for gratitude. In the house in Amsterdam where Anne Frank and her family hid from the Nazis, two charts hang side by side on the wall of the central room. One contains a column of horizontal lines that Otto Frank used to record the growth of his children over the years. On the other chart a series of pins mark the advance of the Allied forces across a map of Europe. In every era, moments of wonder and joy coexist with historical evil and pressing danger.

CHAPTER 6

WHEN GRIEF GIVES
WAY TO HOPE

Heal our wounds, our strength renew;
On our dryness pour your dew;
Wash the stains of guilt away.
Bend the stubborn heart and will;
Melt the frozen, warm the chill;
Guide the steps that go astray.
—"Come Holy Spirit," Sequence for Pentecost

In 1962 the noted American psychiatrist Robert Jay Lifton lived for six months in the city of Hiroshima in order to study the psychological effects of the first nuclear weapon ever used against a human population. Lifton interviewed seventy-five survivors of the atomic bomb. Virtually all those he spoke with reported a similar experience. After the horror of seeing the dead and dying

75

all around, they very quickly ceased to feel. In the words of one witness: "I saw everything but felt nothing." Lifton calls this diminished capacity to feel *psychic numbing*, and names its acute stage *psychic closing off*. Under extreme conditions, such numbing constitutes a useful form of defense, but when it persists, it breeds apathy and despair. Chronic numbing seeps into all areas of life and severs awareness from the energy of emotions.

Several decades after Lifton's classic study, we continue to witness global tragedy and suffering of a magnitude impossible fully to absorb, thereby creating the conditions for widespread apathy. Our feelings pile up the way water pools after a heavy rain, overwhelming soil and drains that cannot take any more. Although a certain distancing from suffering enables us to function on a daily basis, this withdrawal must be balanced with the closeness that is intrinsic to caring relationships. Lifton believes that, in order to engage events so problematic as to defy engagement, we need rituals and symbols that evoke the work of mourning, and the power of an imagination that sustains hope.

As Lifton's research suggests, the work of grieving and imagining is crucial to addressing effectively the ecological destruction, violence, wars, and disease epidemics that endanger the Earth. The felt convictions necessary for action live in emotions such as sadness, fear, anger, wonder, and hope. That is why Jesus directs his message to the heart and offers us vivid images of an alternate world. The Hebrew prophets aim their words at these same affective dynamics. We must likewise attend to them if we are to face our ecological problems honestly.

MOURNING AS PRELUDE TO HOPE

In the early passages of the Book of Jeremiah, the prophet surveys the desolation of Jerusalem following its fall to Babylon, and describes scene upon scene awash with tears and sorrow. Like prophets before and after him, Jeremiah evokes from his hearers a strong visceral response to tragedy, eliciting the affective awareness necessary for conversion. In a passage that speaks eloquently to our own time, he calls his people to lament the silencing of nature: "Take up weeping and wailing for the mountains, / and a lamentation for the pastures of the wilderness, / because they are laid waste so that no one passes through, / and the lowing of cattle is not heard; / both the birds of the air and the animals / have fled and are gone" (9:10–11).

Jeremiah tells his people that only as they grieve their pain will they be able to imagine a new beginning. Issue a summons to the mourning women, he says, and let them raise a lament; let them teach your daughters a dirge and instruct your neighbors in grief (9:17–21). Permission to weep and wail so freely may startle us, but Jeremiah wishes that an even fuller expression of sorrow were possible, that his head was a spring of water and his eyes a fountain of tears so that he could weep day and night for his fallen people (9:1).

Finding expression for our grief enables us to move closer to hope. Which species that have been part of the Earth's story, and are now extinct, do we sense as a loss to the beauty and holiness of the universe? Perhaps we have not noticed, and need our attention alerted to what has vanished: the slender bush wren of New Zealand, the Puerto Rican tree frog, or the lotis blue butterfly of California. What images of global suffering are we carrying? Perhaps a Bangladeshi family surveying the rubble that remains of what was once their home. An Iraqi husband holding the bloody and lifeless body of his wife. Or an Indonesian mother reaching out to the horizon where a tsunami-roiled sea has claimed her children. Not only survivors of such tragedy, but people everywhere must find ways to mourn such loss. Psychic numbing and apathy more readily overtake us when we cannot speak the anguish and anger wrought by suffering. Shrieks and groans, wails and raised fists—these are the spontaneous eruptions of the human spirit in the grip of great grief.

Grief is a restorative process, a way of creating new meaning. Since emotions circulate throughout our bodies and minds, the pain we push away emerges in other forms—irritability, headaches, fatigue, sickness—in spite of efforts to continue with business as usual. Our bodies do the work of our emotions, crying out in despair. A close friend told me that she wanted to let pictures of polar bears threatened by the melting of the Arctic ice shelf seep into her spirit, but the anxiety was too great: "I know they are only one creature, but they are so magnificent." By listening to our feelings and letting them speak, we hear what our fear, anger, and grief are telling us. Only then can we use their resources wisely and find the energy to love again.

One way to do this is to recite a litany that simply names our sorrow over planetary losses, breaking their enormity down into segments we can comprehend. Such a litany might follow this pattern:

> Grieve the decline of the meadowlark, the whip-poor-
> will, and the field sparrow
> deprived of their open grassy habitats
> and mourn for the disappearing forests, once shelter
> of insect and bird.
> Grieve for the Kalahari Bushmen, forced from an
> ancient thriving culture
> into unsanitary, overcrowded, sedentary settlements,
> and mourn the loss of their profound understanding
> of rain.
> Grieve the migrating peoples throughout the globe,
> displaced by violence, war, and natural disasters,
> and mourn their shattered hopes.

Grieve the loss of Earth's seasons, the autumn colors
    that no longer
shimmer, the winter warmth that brings no snow,
and mourn the passing of nature's familiar rhythms.

When leading retreats and workshops I include a simple ritual that speaks to the need for affective engagement with ecological losses. I ask participants to form groups of five or six, to become aware that they are in the presence of God, and then to spend some time together in silence. When ready, each speaks into the silence a word of grief. Then they sit for another period of silence. After this, each speaks into the circle a word of hope. They then close with a group prayer chosen ahead of time. Each person finds strength in the expression of their own sorrow and hope as well as from hearing that of others. Prayer in all its forms, but especially communal prayer, offers ways to articulate what we are feeling. Moreover, listening to others expands and refines what we think of as private emotions.

Sometimes it is anger rather than sorrow that we feel toward others, even God, in light of global tragedy. A primary theme in the Jewish mystical tradition is that such a broken heart is the key to prayer. In the Hasidic tale *Trying to Pray*, Rabbi Dovid Din listens at length to the ranting and raving of a very angry man and then takes him to the Wailing Wall, the only remaining section of the Temple in Jerusalem. When they reach the wall, Rabbi Dovid tells him that it is time to express all the anger he feels toward God. For more than an hour the man strikes the retaining wall with his hands and screams his heart out. After that he begins to cry and cannot stop crying. Then little by little his cries become sobs that turn into prayers. This, the story concludes, is how Reb Dovid taught the man how to pray.

As in this tale, grief often takes the form of anger. Rage, a particularly strong form of anger, results from helplessness. It arises when we watch oil spills spread over pristine waters and habitats, or when we do what we can for the planet on a local level and then learn that massive carbon emissions from coal plants have erased our efforts. Directing the energy of anger frequently calls for involvement in the political process. It means getting clear about what we want and then taking the most direct approach to achieving it. Anger fuels work for justice and, properly channeled, constitutes a major force for saving the planet.

THE PSALMS SHOW US HOW TO PRAY OUR EMOTIONS

We find another resource for the work of mourning in the Book of Psalms. Recited alone or as a community, the psalms have given voice throughout the centuries to the most fundamental of human emotions. Bringing emotions to prayer offers a powerful avenue for their transformation and intensifies our relationship with God. The psalms unapologetically incorporate strong, unvarnished feelings and then turn this sorrow, fear, and anger into gratitude and joy. An impassioned manual of prayer, the Book of Psalms has taught generations of believers how to express even their most painful emotions before God. And lamentation, a shrill and daring cry for help in the midst of pain, occurs not only in the psalms, but in other parts of the Bible as well. Wandering hungry and thirsty in the desert, the Israelites complain to God that they have no water fit to drink (Exod 15:22–25); Job regrets the day he was born in language we might consider too candid for prayer: "Why did I not die at birth, come forth from the womb and expire?" (Job 3:11). These laments encourage us to come to God just as we are. Job's edginess and grit are not out of keeping with the psalms.

The biblical prayers of lament also enable us to recognize the violence and vengeance in our hearts. The so-called *cursing psalms* not only name enemies, they include specific suggestions for what God should do to them: "All my enemies shall be ashamed and struck with terror; / they shall turn back, and in a moment be put to shame" (Ps 6:10). Though we find these calls for divine retribution repugnant, if we are honest we can recognize in them our feelings toward those we see as responsible for despoiling the Earth: "Happy shall they be who pay you back / what you have done to us!" (Ps 137:8). The biblical scholar Walter Brueggemann believes such *venomous passages* in the psalms are to be understood as cathartic, that is, they bring troubling emotions to awareness and expression so that we might move beyond them. When we take these feelings to prayer, we name the depth and intensity of our hurt. Acts of violence need not follow. This language of vengeance is offered to God, and the results are left to the Divine Wisdom.

The psalms show us how not only vengeance, but all difficult emotions are transformed in God's presence. Although laments characteristically begin with a description of pain and a plea for help, they commonly close with expressions of praise, thanks, and an assurance of being heard. For example, Psalm 22 opens with "My God, my God, why have you forsaken me?" (v. 1); later pleads with God, "O my help, come quickly to my aid!" (v. 19); and then culminates in stanzas of praise and thanks for divine deliverance, "You who fear the LORD, praise him!" (v. 23).

Robert Alter, a professor of Hebrew and comparative literature, identifies a feature of biblical poetry that illumines this movement in the psalms. What we might casually hear as repetition is seldom simply a restatement of a theme. We are taken through a powerful crescendo of emotional expression. Ideas and images are intensified and made more specific from one verse to the next. For example, the images in the opening lines of the Book of Lamentations progress from the loneliness of an abandoned city to the immense grief of a widow: "How lonely sits the city that once was full of people! / How like a widow she has become, she that was great among the nations!" (Lam 1:1). This deepening is beautifully illustrated also in two verses from Isaiah that describe a distressed Israel pouring out her prayer: "Like a pregnant woman whose time draws near, she trembles, she screams in her birth pangs" (Isa 26:17). The second part of the verse is not only more concretely focused than the first, but also represents a later moment in the process, from late pregnancy to the midst of labor itself. In praying the psalms, we are to expect something new to happen from one line to the next. We discover that turning to God in tragedy has power to gradually clarify and transform painful emotions, even if this process initially involves a deepening and intensifying of feelings. Prayer in the pattern of the psalms rests on the bedrock of God's love for the world and the steadfastness of divine mercy.

Part of the emotional movement of the psalms is the recognition of our sinfulness and need for repentance. This theme appears especially in the penitential psalms: "Have mercy on me, O God, / according to your steadfast love; / according to your abundant mercy / blot out my transgressions" (Ps 51:1). The psalmist prays, from a place of brokenheartedness, for wisdom, cleansing from sin, and the restoration of joy. Such prayer offers a pattern for the ecological repentance we must embrace, a repentance that refuses to attribute problems simply to others but recognizes greed and violence as residing also in our own hearts. Psalm 32 provides a graphic depiction of the attempt to deny transgressions: "While I kept silence, my body wasted away / through my groaning all day long. / For day and night your hand was heavy upon me; / my strength was dried up as by the heat of summer" (3–4). From this dire position the psalmist turns to an acknowledgment of sin, God's forgiveness, and joy in the steadfastness of divine love.

In all these ways, the psalms pattern for us a kind of prayer that takes us beyond the denial of our destructive impact on the Earth. When we dare to bring to prayer our own fear, acquisitiveness, and potential for violence, we are less likely to project this outward onto others and to see ourselves as fundamentally different from those we label as evil. The seeds of violence and war lie in the human tendency to project onto others the negative qualities in ourselves of which we remain ignorant. The psalms call us to the honest prayer of naming these. Then, held in Divine Wisdom, we can acknowledge the consequences of our way of living and learn to care for the well-being of all species in the cosmos.

JESUS' DREAM OF THE REIGN OF GOD

Maintaining hope in light of catastrophic predictions regarding the planet's future requires alternative visions of a transformed world. For such visions, we rely on the power of the imagination. Imagination plays a central role in stirring hopeful emotions. It does this by offering us a scenario that stands in contrast with the present one, a situation that is different from and seems in fact to contradict current reality. This kind of imaginative paradox forms the core of the gospel message and finds expression especially in the parables.

The central symbol Jesus uses for this hope is the kingdom of God, and it occurs over one hundred and fifty times in the New Testament, most frequently in the synoptic gospels. Because it is a dynamic happening or event rather than the kind of geographical location we associate with historical kingdoms, references to Jesus' kingdom are best translated as the reign of God.

His dream draws on the poetry of the Hebrew prophets. Isaiah depicts a new creation in which God, human beings, and animals dwell together in harmony. Wild and domestic animals—lamb, kid, calf, wolf, leopard, lion, bear—live free of harm and destruction, with a child in their midst. What makes this peace possible? The earth is filled with the knowledge of God "as the waters cover the sea" (11:6–9).

Jesus' parables take the meaning of God's reign right into our hearts. Biblical scholars describe the parables as extended metaphors, stories of ordinary people and events that provide the context for the extraordinary, the transcendent. A new and powerful word from the depths breaks forth in the intervals, surprises, and unusual turns of the parables. In and through the plantings and harvests, budding fig trees, quarreling fathers and sons, women baking bread, seeds growing into shrubs, we discover the presence of God as gift and miracle. We encounter the hidden mystery of the Divine and are challenged by God's reversal of conventional values and tidy schemes. Jesus' parables aim for conversion of heart.

In giving us the parables, Jesus describes the reign of God in such a way that it will alter experience, energize our emotions, and lead to change. As a linguistic form, the parable calls for participants who enter into and experience the word of God, not mere observers who analyze a situation from a safe distance. We frequently read the Bible from an outsider's viewpoint, remaining at some remove from its stories and teachings in order to analyze and apply them to our lives. But conversion of heart happens when we make God's word our home, our dwelling place. Then it changes our perceptions so that we can see the link between Jesus' words and our own decisions. Hearing the word addressed to us in this way calls for the imagination.

A fruitful way to pray the parables incorporates the teaching of Ignatius of Loyola on the use of the imagination. Through imaginative participation, we step inside the gospel parable and become one of those on the scene. Recognizing that a parable is a poetic metaphor, we do not try to solve and explain it. Rather, we let the parable interpret and change us. We simply enter the scene and let it gradually unfold. It sometimes takes fresh and surprising turns.

To pray this way, choose a gospel parable that draws you and prayerfully read it. Then close your eyes and let yourself bring the scene to life. Imagine the details of its setting and action—the sights and sounds, the people present—and then place yourself somewhere in the setting. Perhaps you are one of the main characters, perhaps simply a bystander. For example, in the parable of the vineyard, become one of the laborers who has worked a full day and who expects to be paid more than those hired later (Matt 20:1–15). While waiting in line for your pay, feel the evening cool after the scorching heat of the day. Notice how stained your hands are from the labor. Cast an eye about at the other workers, the manager, and the landlord. Finally your turn comes. You discover that you will be paid the same as everyone else. How do you react? Notice how you feel about your own pay as well as the amount given to others. Spend some time in a reign of God that disrupts your notion of fairness. What would it mean for you to live according to the parable's vision and values?

Parables unsettle, but offer no precise blueprint for action. Though we are not told exactly what to do, we know the direction to take, for Jesus' ministry brings the reign of God into our midst. As in the parables of the prodigal son (Luke 15:11–32) and the forgiving owner (Matt 18:23–35), Jesus shows us a startling breadth of mercy and forgiveness. We glimpse the unexpected realm of God, so different from our current arrangements and so full of abundant grace and forgiveness. The hope engendered by Jesus' dream allows people everywhere to imagine life without its present overlay of suffering; it assures them that suffering is not a good in itself, not something to be borne without protest. Rather than explain this reign of God, Jesus illustrates its coming with his life and actions. He lives always in God's presence, moves against sickness and evil of every kind, brims with compassion for anyone who suffers, and struggles to bring about right relationships. He shows us that the way to believe in a future of love and justice is to live it in the here and now—to think and act as if the reign of God were already in our midst.

THE REIGN OF GOD IN JESUS' NATURE PARABLES

In announcing the reign of God Jesus draws on what medieval theologians called the book of nature. He not only includes human experience, but uses as his starting point dying fig trees, vineyards, straying sheep, and seeds sown in promising as well as rugged locations. In this way we come to realize that the reign of God includes nature as well as human history. Like those parables that portray human activity, Jesus' nature metaphors convey a surprisingly extravagant hope.

The fourth chapter of Mark's gospel contains no less than three seed parables—seed sown on rocky and good soil, seeds that sprout and grow while the sower sleeps, and the tiny mustard seed that grows into a large shrub with branches large enough to shelter birds from the sun. Along with their grounding in the book of nature, these parables convey two teachings about the reign of God that are especially significant for an ecological spirituality. First, although our efforts are important to the coming of the reign, we are not finally responsible for its arrival. God is. Second, God brings unexpected results from small beginnings.

The poet Jerome McElroy captures the parables' sturdy promise for all creation in "The Habit of Hope." What is hope?

> It's the spine of the crocus
> creasing the tombstone
> building to bloom alone after dusk
> with woods asleep and the world unaware.

The Spirit's presence in all creation's fragile and partial efforts appears as well in the parable of the mustard seed. Jesus wants to ready us for the coming of God's reign. But rather than call attention to the stately cedars of Lebanon, he turns to a seemingly insignificant mustard plant, what some Semitic villagers might call an invasive weed. Once again we have a largesse of grace issuing from an unpromising beginning.

Many who care about our planet struggle to believe that their small actions can make a difference. Recently a remarkable story appeared in our local newspaper. It reported on the huge role stormwater damage plays in polluting Puget Sound. While we fear the consequences of large oil spills such as the 1989 Exxon Valdez accident in Alaska, which spilled eleven million gallons of oil, stormwater from roads, parking lots, and other areas sends eight million gallons of petroleum annually into the Sound. Not just industry, but all that we do in our cars and homes contributes to the problem. This story reads like a parable in reverse—immense destruction issuing from small actions. But it points the way out of the problem, as well.

As we assess the scope of our global problems, Christian hope may promise slim power against larger forces. Yet the gospels counsel a way rooted in its parables: action born of love but grounded in the promises of God. A new generation of Latin American liberation theologians addresses this issue from the perspective of their own historical struggles with oppression.

They recognize that many of the economic and political changes desired by the first generation of liberation theologians have not come about. For example, Korean-born theologian Jung Mo Sung believes that the Exodus paradigm used by these earlier thinkers overestimated the possibility of bringing about liberation in history. The crucifixion and resurrection of Jesus offer a different paradigm. Jesus' experience exemplifies the indignation experienced by so much of humanity, but it also points to the limits of history. The paradox of a defeated messiah empowers each individual in the Christian community to struggle against suffering in spite of the many defeats we may encounter. Although God's reign will come about only in God's time, incremental changes that improve the lives of the oppressed can and must happen even now.

Hope in the power of small actions also arises from the interrelatedness of the world's problems. In an interconnected universe, social and environmental issues are knit so tightly into one system that following any concern takes us full circle: Globalization feeds consumption, and consumption increases the use of carbon fuels. Carbon fuels contribute to climate change, which in turn becomes a factor in global justice and injustice. An exercise that can be done in small faith communities, or during workshops and retreats, shows how these connections actually intensify the positive significance of individual action.

A group is asked to brainstorm about the problems the world faces today, naming them out loud. As each problem is identified, it is recorded in random order on a blackboard or sheet of newsprint until it is full. Members of the group are asked to silently ponder the list and then draw a picture of the feelings it evokes. Each titles his or her drawing and shares it with one other person. Next the group focuses back on the board and decides which of the identified problems are connected. As they call out that water shortages are related to violence, or that AIDS in Africa is connected to illiteracy, which in turn stems from poverty, an arrow is drawn between the related issues. Soon, connecting arrows cover the board. Each member of the group then chooses one problem that he or she feels drawn to work on and studies the arrows attached to it. It becomes clear that working on one problem affects every other. We need not do everything, but only find our particular way of contributing to the reign of God.

At our present crossroads, when the future of our planet truly is at stake, we can act with the assurance that our contributions are important. Reliance on the power of small actions to provide a way out of fear and hopelessness was one of the great gifts of the nineteenth-century Carmelite Thérèse of Lisieux. The circumstances of her life could have left her in a state of despair. One of nine children, of whom only five survived, Thérèse lost her mother a few months after her birth. She herself died of tuberculosis when she was only twenty-four. But Thérèse had a deep conviction that small actions done with love change everything; every act of love somehow strengthens the universe, and every act of hatred weakens it. Her spirituality influenced both Mother Teresa of Calcutta and Dorothy Day. In fact, when ordinary people asked what they could do, Dorothy Day pointed to the little way of St. Thérèse, a path that Day thought was misunderstood and unfairly despised: "She began with working for peace in her own heart, and willing to love where love was difficult, and so she grew in love, and increased the sum total of love in the world, not to speak of peace."

Hope is born when we imagine together. In fact, hope cannot be achieved alone; rather, it is an act of collaboration or mutuality. The private imagination soon reaches the end of its resources. We cannot address singly every global challenge, for they are too numerous and overwhelming. What can be done? A sense of the possible emerges when a community—church, nation, two people—develop hope in one another, hope that they will receive help from each other.

Drawing on his research into organizations dedicated either to the environment or to social justice, causes which he considers inseparable, Paul Hawken suggests a way we might strengthen our communal imagination. In his book *Blessed Unrest: How the Largest Movement in the World Came into Being and Why No One Saw It Coming*, Hawken cites over one million nonprofits and one hundred million people who work daily for the preservation and restoration of life on Earth. These range from multimillion nonprofits to single-person dot-causes. Hawken believes we need an intertwining of these groups that constitute a movement from the bottom up, one with no name, leader, or location. Though war and political conflicts more often make the news, the groups Hawken identifies actually comprise the largest movement in the world, and the most powerful—not in terms of weapons, but in terms of people's hearts and determination. Simply knowing that all these groups exist, that we are not alone but labor in the company of many others, buoys hope. They are the branches of the tiny mustard seed, grown large enough to shelter planetary hope.

CHAPTER 7

WE HAVE HERE
A LASTING HOME

I don't want to end up simply having visited this world.

—Mary Oliver

🌿 In prayers, hymns, and conversations we often separate heaven and Earth into two realms. Heaven exists somewhere above us; Earth lies here below. When trouble strikes, comfort comes from the assurance that we are but pilgrims on this planet, making our way to our true destination, a better land where there will be no further suffering, no more tears. Human beings in every era yearn for the promise enfolded in the term *heaven*. But viewing the Earth as simply a way station to a heavenly destination risks turning creation into a throw-away object, undercutting our responsibility for its future. Splitting heaven and Earth apart also overlooks the fact that the divine presence is woven into the fiber of the universe. The natural world is intrinsically sacred and valuable, not simply a means to an end. Ecological writing insists that we belong to this universe. But just as black holes in the galaxy devour starlight, so evil eats away at trust in Earth as our true home. To ring true to experience, the affirmation that we are at home on the Earth must take into account the suffering and death found throughout creation. The multilayered image of *home* evokes for me not only comfort, but a memory of profound family grief. Five years ago my husband's twenty-six-year-old niece, Karla, shot herself in the heart. Upheld by the unstinting efforts of her parents and twin brother, Karla battled a severe form of bipolar disorder for eight years before the disease finally prevailed. Winsome, beautiful, and immensely talented, Karla brought to the struggle all the spiritual resources she could muster. At the time of her funeral and during the years since her death, Karla's family has chosen to be completely open about her illness and the circumstances of her death, founding the Karla Smith Foundation to help families in similar circumstances.

The morning after Karla's wake, her mother and the rest of her extended family gathered around her open casket for a last good-bye before it was closed. Her mother explained that when Karla was little and could not sleep, she used to sing a lullaby to soothe her. She wanted to sing that song to her now. In the midst of her immeasurable sorrow, she somehow found a voice for its lyrics: "O give me a home, where the buffalo roam, where the deer and the antelope play. Where seldom is heard a discouraging word, and the skies are not cloudy all day." The other family members, comfortable from childhood with the melody and its harmonies, joined in "Home on the Range." In those moments the former lullaby was transformed into a blessing for Karla, becoming now a prayer for a peace larger than anything she had been able to find in her short life. Its vision of hope included a peaceful natural world, a renewed creation marked by the playful freedom Karla so loved.

When those close to us endure unrelieved pain and grief, when stories of torture and violence fill the media, when life on Earth seems unbearable, how do we avoid an imaginary flight into heaven to escape it all? How do we formulate a hope that is firmly fastened to our place in the cosmos? How do we bring together heaven and Earth in such a way that our sense of the sacred and our resolve to care for the Earth remain strong in face of creation's terrible need for redemption? In response to these questions Christian spirituality invites us to meditate on three metaphors: Earth as home, resurrection as transformation, and redemption as new creation. Each offers themes for a holistic spirituality, one that heals the split between Earth and heaven, matter and spirit, creation and salvation.

EARTH AS HOME

Exploration into space allows us to view our planet Earth as our one and only home. We now have striking images of it suspended in stellar darkness, situated amid the approximately one hundred billion galaxies of the universe. Viewing Earth as home invites us to a new way of thinking about our place in the universe. We belong, together with all other species, to one cosmos. Earth is humanity's habitat, but it is also the dwelling place or habitat of every other being. At one level, then, the image of *home* enlarges, in terms of time and space, what it means to be a human being. It emphasizes our connection to all creation and our responsibility to care for it as we would a home. It also evokes gratitude for the essential nurturance we receive from the universe, for the countless moments in which the natural world births, feeds, shelters, clothes, and heals us.

The mathematical cosmologist Brian Swimme provides poetry for this perspective. Isolation and loneliness are false cosmic states, he believes. For we were born from the Earth community and are deeply bonded to it, relatives of atoms and bacteria, roses and sparrows, insects and whales, galaxies and planets. We need to find imaginative ways to experience this intimacy. Every child should know that she is the energy of the sun and feel her face shining with the joy found in this primordial relationship. Sunlight streams through the oceans and hums in the forests. We learn from the sun's generosity in bestowing energy, discovering in this underlying impulse of the universe our own urge to contribute to the wider community. Swimme tells us that to contemplate the solar system in which this immense Earth is swung around its massive cosmic partner, the sun, "is to touch an ocean of wonder as you take a first step into inhabiting the actual universe and solar system and Earth." Yes, we are pilgrims, but in each moment of our journey we are filled with light from the beginning of time, from the birthplace of the universe fifteen billion light-years away. Suffused with this vision of the universe, we might be moved to pause on our journey, lifting our faces to the sun to take in the energy of God's love.

This poetic portrayal of our cosmic home holds implications for action right in the midst of everyday life. If we lose sight of how we are bonded to the Earth, we are apt to split apart our concern for personal and public space. We will lavish care on our clothing, cars, and houses, while allowing the public spaces that surround us—wetlands and forests, streams and oceans, sidewalks and neighborhoods—to deteriorate. We wash our cars with toxic chemicals, unaware that in our singular focus on having a shining vehicle we are killing fish in the streams nearby. We adorn our yards and decks with flowers, but litter sidewalks, parks, and green spaces. Efforts to create renewable energy, such as wind farms, stumble when we protest the presence of wind turbines near our property.

Theologian Ivone Gabara tells how the women and men of her Brazilian neighborhood struggle hard for survival, but do not always realize the connection between their children's health and the chickens they sell on the corner or the dirty water running through the streets after streetcleaning: "The streets turn into a public garbage dump. On the inside, their houses are generally neat, but the street, the collective space, is practically a no-man's-land." The poor have very little access to public services and therefore do not care for public space as if it belonged to them. Richer neighborhoods are cleaner and better cared for, while poorer areas are frequently neglected. Impoverishment of the land in Asia, Africa, and Latin America means that women must walk twice as far each day to gather wood or find water; it means that children die in shantytowns from lack of food and clean water. Though Earth is our home, it is not yet the household God has in mind.

It is often poor and indigenous people, however, who best know how to treat the Earth as home. Poor women of Latin America, although excluded from basic services such as health and education, understand inherently how to care for all forms of life, and are least likely to destroy the environment that is so important to their extended families, neighborhoods, and communities. By necessity they do not throw away a coat or pair of shoes that can be passed on to others; they conserve electricity, taking advantage of daylight as long as possible to knit or sew; they terrace land so that it waters trees and gardens rather than causing erosion. In the shantytowns and countryside that surround the cities, nothing is regarded as garbage—not tires that can be used as flower beds or water rafts, or discarded boxes and containers that can hold unpackaged food or nails and bolts. In spite of the injustice that creates their poverty, they remain guardians of the Earth's resources.

Like all images, that of Earth as home holds many levels of sometimes contradictory meanings. We belong to the cosmos, but not all dwell equitably within it. The New Testament Book of Revelation contains insights into the contrasting landscapes we inhabit. Revelation has been interpreted in many ways, at times leading to ecological destruction and disregard for women and for this world. But in it we also discover a tale of two cities with an Earth-centered vision for the future.

We know the author of Revelation simply as John, but probably not the same John who wrote the gospel. His message is addressed to urban Christians living in the prosperous port of Ephesus and other Asia Minor cities. John wrote to encourage these Christians and to urge them to greater justice and hope. He lays before them the rival cities of Babylon and New Jerusalem and invites them to leave behind the evil empire of Babylon—a metaphor for Rome, the empire under which they live—and enter the city of justice and well-being, the New Jerusalem. In chapters 17 and 18, Revelation presents Babylon as a desolate landscape, a site of ecological devastation. It is a world of commerce, of buying and selling, a city frenetically piling up wealth. In chapters 21 and 22, it portrays the New Jerusalem, where life and its essentials come as God's gift, even to those who cannot pay for them. In God's new city there will be no more death, mourning, weeping, or pain.

Near the New Jerusalem flows a river of life. Trees on the river's banks thrive, boasting leaves that promise reconciliation and healing for the nations. Here people are not lifted from the Earth in rapture, as they are in some apocalyptic thinking; rather, God comes down from heaven and makes a home on Earth, pitching a tent among us: "See, the dwelling of God is among mortals. God will dwell with them as their God; they will be his people, and God's very self will be with them..." (21:3). In this holy city, God's presence transforms space into the new creation.

Here we have an Earth-centered vision of our home with God—a city with abundant trees and fresh water for all, a metropolis of beauty and justice whose gates are open. The New Jerusalem heralds a healed landscape and reconciled nations, the integration of nature with urban life. New Testament scholar Barbara Rossing sees Revelation's message as a future we can catch sight of even now: "In every tree, every river, every city, we can glimpse God's holy city dawning in our midst." Letting visions of the New Jerusalem fire our imaginations keeps hope alive and commits us to the flourishing of all creatures in God's household.

Bringing the image of Earth as home into our prayer allows it gradually to convert our imaginations. We might make it a part of grace at community meals.

> We give thanks, Divine Wisdom, for the rich array
> of relatives who share our home.
> We praise you for the falling rain, the fruitful fields,
> and every green growing thing.
> As we journey with all creation toward full
> communion in you,
> teach us to reverence other creatures as beloved
> members of your household. Amen

Or we might take time on a walk or at the end of the day to raise our awareness that Earth is home: When was I most attuned today to the length and breadth of the boundaries I call home? In what moments did I walk lightly on the Earth, grateful for its gifts and mindful of my bond with the universe? Do I treat public space with the care I give my private possessions? How might I address the way public space reflects the gap between the rich and the poor of the world?

RESURRECTION AS TRANSFORMATION

The twentieth-century biblical scholar Raymond Brown makes clear in his study of Jesus' resurrection that what happened to Jesus' body is of major significance for the issues of our time. Future possibilities for creation are patterned on what God has already done in Jesus: "Will the material world pass away and all be made anew, or will somehow the world be transformed and changed into the city of God?" The answer determines whether the body of the Earth, to which our bodies are intrinsically linked, has permanent or merely passing importance. If the body is of only fleeting significance, why bother to care for the Earth or for bodies around the globe? Like old clothes destined to be discarded, they can be used and cast aside. According to Brown, the question of the bodily resurrection is not simply an example of Christian curiosity; rather it is related to the major theological theme of·God's ultimate purpose in creating. The bodily resurrection of Jesus indicates that God's intentions for the Earth, the relationship between old and new creation, are best captured by the model of transformation.

Several New Testament passages are important to this theme of resurrection as transformation. Among them are the gospel accounts of Jesus' appearances to his disciples. Amid the variety of details found in these appearance stories, one common theme persists, even though it goes against expectations. When the risen Jesus appears to his disciples, they have trouble recognizing him. He is the same Jesus with whom they walked and shared meals, but now somehow so different that they do not know him. In each Easter story there are moments of not knowing and then suddenly recognizing Jesus. Consider, for example, Jesus' appearance to Mary Magdalene as told near the end of John's gospel. It is just before dawn when Mary peers into Jesus' tomb and finds it empty. She is distraught as she takes the measure of her loss, and when Jesus himself stands before her, she does not know him but mistakes him for the gardener. Mary answers Jesus' question, "Whom do you seek?" with a tearful reporting of Jesus' missing body and laments that someone must have taken him away. Jesus says to her, "Mary!" Now called by name, she realizes who he is.

The other accounts of Jesus' resurrection appearances contain the same theme. Jesus walks alongside two of his disciples on their way to Emmaus. "While they were talking and discussing, Jesus himself came near and went with them, but their eyes were kept from recognizing him" (Luke 24:15–16). Only after Jesus and the two travelers have a long talk and share a meal do they recognize him. Then he vanishes from their midst.

What is the meaning of this continuity and discontinuity, this identity and difference, between the Jesus the disciples knew during his ministry and the Jesus they encounter in the resurrection appearances? Paul struggles with this question as he addresses Christians in the vibrant Greek city of Corinth. When Paul writes, it is about 56 CE, not long after Jesus' crucifixion and resurrection appearances, but the Corinthians' questions are contemporary: How can a body decay in the ground and yet rise again? What sort of body could that possibly be? In other words, what does it mean for one thing to become something else?

Paul answers by describing a different kind of bodily existence. A grain dies and finds life again in a different body, and there is continuity between the seed and the plant. Paul suggests that something like this happens in resurrection. His comparison is perhaps easier to grasp while driving past fields of wheat, golden and glorious in the late afternoon sunlight. The swaying stalks do not resemble rotting seed, but that is what they sprang from. "So it is with the resurrection of the dead. What is sown is perishable, what is raised is imperishable. It is sown in dishonor, it is raised in glory. It is sown in weakness, it is raised in power. It is sown a physical body, it is raised a spiritual body" (1 Cor 15:42–44).

By means of his seed analogy, Paul makes several crucial points. In resurrection, an open-ended transformation is happening. The sprouting wheat indeed differs from the bare seed, but it is not entirely different. Metamorphosis, or change, always includes the issue of ongoing identity, for if there is no connection between past and present reality, we encounter simply two different things, not transfiguration. This kind of hoped-for metamorphosis is movingly conveyed by the many chrysalises and butterflies painted by children about to die in the concentration camp in Theresienstadt, paintings preserved today in the Jewish museum in Prague.

In trying to convey both change and ongoing connection with what came before, Paul calls the resurrected body a *spiritual* body, but it has always been difficult to understand exactly what he means. One clue is that the *spiritual* person Paul talks about in the rest of his letter to the Corinthians is not some sort of ethereal reality, but an ordinary person who has been made new by the Spirit of God. Paul is not thinking of a disembodied soul that escapes death. Death is real, and the contrast between this present body and what Paul calls the spiritual body is as great as that between a decaying seed and a sheaf of wheat. Further, he wants to make clear that the resurrected body is not simply a resuscitated dead body. For him, the human person is a unity. The *whole* person moves into a new Spirit-filled existence and then is changed again in death. Paul is groping for redemption language that entails not just body, and not just spirit, but both.

From Paul's message, along with that of the gospels, we learn that matter has a future. The Spirit is at work transforming the entire universe. As the firstborn of the new creation, the resurrected Christ promises a resurrected creation. The gospel stories of continuity and discontinuity—of being mistaken for a ghost and then sharing food, of not being recognized and then being known, of appearance and disappearance within closed rooms—these all indicate the ongoing significance of the material world, for they show that Christ's body has been changed, not destroyed. They affirm the importance of the material in all its physical, touchable reality.

The theme of bodily transfiguration is developed in additional ways in John's gospel, where sapiential or wisdom themes dominate the discussion of resurrection. John sees Jesus as the Wisdom of God dwelling in our midst. In the opening chapter of his gospel, he describes Jesus, in language taken from biblical wisdom literature, as the Word made flesh. John's opening hymn proclaims that all that belongs to the history of creation exists through this Word (1:1–14). John's interpretation of Jesus' resurrection also draws on the Wisdom of Solomon and is deeply grounded in Hebrew sensibility. For the Jewish imagination, life without the body, even after death, would be inconceivable. In John's gospel, the terms *flesh*, *blood*, and *body*, which might in English denote simply *parts* of a person, refer here instead to the *whole* person viewed under one or another different aspect. So for John, resurrection means that the whole embodied person experiences life in God—now lived partially, but in the future found in its fullness. The disciples ask, "Where is the Lord?" and the answer is that he is glorified and with God. His going away brings about a promise of mutual interiority with his disciples; in the Spirit he will dwell with them and in them. This is an embodied presence, the spiritual present in the material. His disciples are also his real presence, his body in the world (John 14—15).

When the risen Jesus appears to his disciples in the house into which they had locked themselves out of fear (John 20:19–30), he invites Thomas to feel the wounds in his hand and side. Just as Jesus invites his disciple to touch the death marks on his scarred body, so we are invited to touch the scars on the Earth's body—the slashes left from the clear cutting of forests; the empty landscapes now missing birds, plants, and animals as they become extinct. Easter proclaims the promise that these scars—along with all others that we bear on our human and Earth bodies—will be healed. This includes scarred countries like El Salvador, where 80 percent of the natural vegetation has been destroyed and only 6 percent of the original forests remain, where people struggle for liberation from the economic and political structures that have brought about this environmental degradation. Belief in the bodily resurrection of Jesus thus provides a pivotal motivation for our care of creation. God will not abandon this scarred Earth; nor should we. The matter of this world will be the transfigured matter of the world to come.

REDEMPTION AS NEW CREATION

The letters of the apostle Paul were read aloud to gatherings of Christians in cities around the Roman Empire. His message to Christians in the powerful city of Rome is the longest of his epistles, and the only one addressed to a church he did not found. Because of its length, it stands first among his letters, but it might also claim this position on the basis of the enormous influence it has exercised in the history of Christianity. Many of the letter's themes jostle for attention, but here we will focus on just one—the solidarity of humanity with the rest of creation in its longing for redemption.

Though he gives the topic only a brief space in his larger discussion, Paul speaks movingly of creation's longing to be freed from suffering and decay. It leans toward this liberation with eager yearning. All creation shares the expectations of believers as they wait in anguish and hope: "We know that the whole creation has been groaning in labor pains until now; and not only the creation, but we ourselves, who have the first fruits of the Spirit, groan inwardly while we wait for adoption, the redemption of our bodies" (Rom 8:22–23).

Like the Hebrew prophets Isaiah (13:8) and Jeremiah (4:31), Paul uses birth pangs as a metaphor for the time of suffering that will usher in a new age. He vividly portrays the struggle of the entire universe, not just human beings, for the redemption promised by God.

In her book *Our Mother Saint Paul*, Beverly Gaventa traces the way Paul uses maternal imagery to talk about his apostolic labors, referring at times to himself as mother, as in his letter to the Galatians: "My little children, for whom I am again in the pain of childbirth until Christ is formed in you, I wish I were present with you now and could change my tone, for I am perplexed about you" (4:19–20). Gaventa shows how, in this passage as well as others, Paul identifies his apostolic work with the apocalyptic expectations of the entire created order. In Romans 8:23 he is indicating the cosmic horizon of the new creation that God is bringing to birth. Paul insists that the Spirit of God is reclaiming the cosmos from the power of sin and death, bringing hope even in the midst of its suffering and pain. Despair and doubt are the birth pangs of this new creation. Creation and redemption are not split into two opposing actions of God, for both form one divine movement. In God's redeeming action we encounter creation, and in the liberating power of redemption we find the gift of the Creator.

The renowned Canadian artist Emily Carr brings the feel of this Romans passage to life in her paintings. In her lifelong search for God, Carr learned the mysterious spirituality of nature from the First Nations' people during her frequent trips to Indian villages. But she also sought to find harmony between her Christian faith and the spiritual power she experienced in the natural world. Her paintings express many of God's attributes— peace, joy, and strength—and frequently have as their subject trees and the forest. Carr often voiced dismay over the leveling of trees to make room for a development, or the clear cutting of a forest for timber. In her journals, she refers to the tree stumps left behind as "screamers": "These are the unsawn last bits, the cry of the tree's heart, wrenching and tearing apart just before she gives that sway and the dreadful groan of falling." With a poet and artist's sensibility, Carr depicts concretely a creation that is awaiting redemption.

The groaning of a creation that longs for liberation is heard in human as well as nonhuman experience. The immediate feelings of an oppressed people are conveyed with poetic intensity and vivid imagery in African American spirituals, gospels, and hymns, as, for example, well-known songs like "Sometimes I Feel Like A Motherless Child" and "Nobody Knows the Trouble I've Seen":

Nobody knows de trouble I seen
Nobody knows but Jesus
Nobody knows de trouble I've had
Glory hallelu!

Though some have interpreted this religious music as focused on a future salvation in heaven, the details of daily physical misery—"My knee bones am aching, / My body's rackin' with pain"—suggest a desire for freedom in this world as well as the next. In keeping with their African heritage, the slaves considered the separation between these two realities to be narrow. Their God was personal and concerned, and their music united this world and the world to come. Further, there was almost always a latent or overt protest and sense of impending freedom in their religious songs.

> O Freedom! O Freedom!
> O Freedom, I love thee!

African American religious music reflects the suffering inflicted by relentless cruelty, but it also transmits a fundamentally different worldview—one of sustenance, communal bonding, promise, and hope.

Viewed within a larger cosmic worldview, the groaning of creation that Paul describes connects with the evolutionary promise found in the universe's fourteen-billion-year story. Suffering, loss, and death have always been part of the ongoing creation of life. Seen through an evolutionary lens, creation's yearning for fullness arises from the fact that the universe remains unfinished. Yet, in spite of all its failures and tragedies, the cosmos, including both Earth and humanity, is being called to fuller modes of being. Human sin consists in our resistance to the Divine Wisdom that seeks to fashion creation ever more fully into the unity and uniqueness found in the divine life. Through such refusals we continue to contribute to its anguish.

The epistle to the Colossians also tells us that redemption is intended to reach the whole cosmos, not just humanity. Through Jesus' death and resurrection God reconciled "all things, whether on earth or in heaven" (1:20), inaugurating the transformation of all creation. This hymn to the risen Christ, modeled on Wisdom as is the opening to John's gospel, celebrates the cosmic Christ as both the source and goal of creation (Col 1:15–20). Similar themes appear in the letter to the Ephesians, where we learn that all things will be gathered up in the risen Christ (1:9–10).

Had the Jesuit paleontologist Teilhard de Chardin lived to share in contemporary discussions of these epistles, he would have rejoiced. They place Christ at the heart of cosmic redemption, as he had hoped to do with his own writings. Teilhard saw redemption as the continuation of creation, and he emphasized Christ's function in the cosmic and social realms, rather than exclusively in the personal redemption of individuals. Though his science was limited to the insights of his time, he envisaged salvation not as an escape from the world, but as the world's completion and sanctification.

Our hope is centered then in the promise that Earthly life will be changed, not destroyed. We will be redeemed with this Earth, not apart from it, and will rise with all other living beings—persons, animals, trees, plants. The Wisdom that creates is also the Wisdom that redeems. This imbues the present world with immense significance as both our present and future home.

CHAPTER 8

CONTEMPLATION AND
THE CARE OF CREATION

Eventually only our sense of the sacred will save us.
—Thomas Berry

Although she lived before the current ecology movement took hold, the British religious writer Evelyn Underhill dedicated her life to bringing about the transformation now recognized as essential to our planet's future. One of the most widely read spiritual authors of the twentieth century, Underhill realized that only contemplation can slake our thirst and fulfill our potential. We need a transfigured consciousness to address society's problems, and she was convinced that it comes about through what she called *adherence to God*. She used terms such as *worship* and *adoration* for this relationship with the Divine, which at its core she saw as love.

Author of a classic study on mysticism, Underhill believed that the great mystics point the way for the rest of us, and the passion of her mature work was the contemplative life of ordinary women and men. In support of this, she introduced spiritual direction and retreats to her Anglican community and sought to remove the misunderstandings that paint contemplation as elitist and esoteric. From her studies she was familiar with the visions and voices we associate with mysticism, but she insisted that they were not the heart of it. Holiness belongs to everyone, not only those in cloister or monastery, and it represents the true human calling. Prayer and action are inextricably linked, as she showed by her weekly presence in the North Kensington slums and her embrace of pacifism during World War II. She struggled with the limits of institutional religion but came to see that it provided a protection for personal religious experience and a context for her ministry.

Underhill lived from 1875 to 1941, and her lifespan makes her a contemporary of both Thérèse of Lisieux and Teilhard de Chardin. Like Thérèse, she believed that prayer so sanctifies ordinary moments that they can change the world. And though she lacked Teilhard's cosmic vision, Underhill appreciated the power of science and technology, and shared his belief in the movement of the heart that takes us to the fully real. With Thérèse and Teilhard, Underhill saw that prayer alters not only the person who prays, but the universe as well. We can wade with wisdom into the messiness of our troubled planet, even into the horror of its violence and evil, when anchored in the love of God and all that God loves.

What would happen if we gave priority to contemplation, if we taught it in our schools and churches? This question raised by Underhill's life and work can be heard in many quarters today. It can seem foolhardy to rely on something so apparently impractical to tackle the alarming issues before us. But unless we undergo a transformation of consciousness, we will address problems such as climate change from a familiar consumer mindset. The New Testament names the transformation we need *metanoia*, a term usually translated as conversion. It implies a great turning around, and contemplation is its foundation.

RECEIVING AS A WAY OF LOVING

When faced with a crisis, our first response is to ask what we can do. Paradoxically, the contemplation that grounds wise action is a form of deep receptivity. The contemplative mode of awareness asks that we listen primarily with the heart rather than the mind, awaiting what is to be revealed, the way a sponge soaks up water or a sunflower lifts its face to the sun. All subsequent thinking and acting are shaped by the connections discovered in such prayer. It inserts us experientially into the relational world described by current science and theology. In the absence of such an experience of deep interconnectedness, theories of a universe in which all creatures live in communion with God and one another risk remaining abstractions.

Contemplation has piqued the interest of psychology as well as theology and generated research into the kind of awareness it entails. Studies of contemplation's psychological dynamics indicate why its revival bears so much significance for an ecological age. According to this research, two contrasting stances characterize the way we interact with the world around us. Sometimes we actively manage, arrange, and direct what is happening. We make lists, call prospective clients, assemble the parts of a jetliner, and pour the foundations of a new home. In all these activities we are striving to meet personal goals, operating in a rational, verbal, and linear mode. Our boundary perception—

our sense of the edges separating us from others—is clear, and our energies are focused on the task before us.

At other times we primarily take in or receive reality, as when we listen to the story of a grieving friend, take a walk in the woods, view the paintings in a museum, or look for the constellations in a night sky. We operate in a more holistic, intuitive, and nonlinear way, one organized around the intake of our environment. Our attention is more diffuse, and subject/object boundaries are transcended. We have a sense of solidarity with other human beings and with the universe.

The psychiatrist Arthur Diekmann compares these two modes of awareness respectively to a New York cab driver making his way to the airport at rush hour and a monk walking quietly in an abbey garden. The cab driver concentrates on immediate traffic conditions and chooses maneuvers that promise the most effective route to the airport. The monk, meanwhile, is free to experience his relationship with the surrounding grass, flowers, and sky without the need to change them. He can take in the whole panorama of his environment, and through it enter into communion with God and nature. Wonder belongs to this receptive mode of awareness.

Both the cab driver and the monk reside within each of us, and in truth we need both. The first, or active, mode of awareness leads us to manufacture homes and build cities, to navigate the oceans and care for our families, to analyze and address the problems devastating the Earth community. This focus produces results, but it can lead to a kind of tunnel vision that blinds us to larger realities. The second or nonpragmatic mode initially regards other realities as they exist in themselves. When we contemplate the sun and moon, we are not thinking of conquering space; we are rather opening ourselves to the Mystery the skies reveal. This receptive mode takes us to play, paintings, symphonies, cosmic musings, and a sense of kinship with all creation.

We might fear that if we encourage a contemplative approach to reality, we will simply drift about in life, like branches swayed by every passing breeze. But receptivity need not impede agency; it rather ensures that our actions spring from a clearer concern for the whole. This is the insight expressed in the effort all healthy spirituality makes to unite contemplation and action. In contemplation we listen for a deeper Wisdom than that immediately apparent. When we make time to first take in the environment, we are less likely to regard creation as simply there to serve our needs, to be manipulated to feed our factories and contribute to corporate profit.

This changed perception is beautifully expressed by the clinical psychologist Anne Benvenuti as she writes about her relationship with her brown and white Jack Russell terrier, Molly Brown. Because her dog loved her so intensely, Anne says, she felt compelled to love her back. That meant learning to listen to Molly, discovering who she was and what she needed, finding out what it means to be a dog. Her relationship with this fifteen-pound dog restored Anne to the universe and taught her that we cannot be human without the guidance of the nonhuman world. She began to develop accurate empathy, to see the universe not as a commodity for our consumption, but as companion, friend, and teacher. When we love any one thing, Benvenuti notes, we love the entire universe that contains it.

A Hasidic tale reflects how this way of listening lets prayer simply emerge from the heart, how it makes prayer available to everyone. As the story goes, one Yom Kippur when Rabbi Isaac Luria was praying in the synagogue, an angel whispered in his ear that there was a man whose prayer had reached the highest heavens. The angel told him the man's name and the city where he lived, so the rabbi set out to find him, for he wanted to know the secret of his prayer. He looked for him first among the learned in the House of Study, and then searched amid the din of the market. There he learned that the only man by that name was a poor farmer who lived in the mountains. So the rabbi climbed the hills, and when he reached his hut, the man invited the rabbi to come in. When the rabbi inquired about the secret of his prayer, the man was very surprised. "But rabbi," he replied, "I am afraid that I cannot pray. For I cannot read. All I know are the letters of the alphabet from *aleph* to *yod*." This astonished the rabbi, and he asked, "What did you do on Yom Kippur?" The man replied, "I went to the synagogue. And when I saw how intently everyone around me was praying, my heart broke. And I began to recite all that I know of the alphabet. And I said in my heart: 'Dear God, take these letters and form them into prayers for me that will rise up like the scent of honeysuckle. For that is the most beautiful scent that I know.' And that is what I said with all my strength, over and over."

TWO PATHS TO CONTEMPLATING THE COSMOS

Paradox defines our experience of God in another way. We know that God is wholly other and invisible. Yet we also discern traces of God everywhere. The Divine is revealed but veiled, known but unknown. The Bible returns repeatedly to this alternating presence and absence of God, a presence that arrives as nonconsuming fire and sustaining manna during the Israelites' sojourn in the desert, and an absence that evokes the psalmist's plea, "Hide not your face from us." Two traditional contemplative paths name the way this paradox appears in the spiritual life. Known by terms drawn from their Greek origins, they are designated the *apophatic* or negative way, and the *kataphatic* or affirmative path, and they describe not only approaches to prayer, but all human attempts to know and talk about God. Christian theology and prayer move back and forth between naming God and being reduced to silence before an encompassing Mystery, between finding God in all creation and acknowledging the profound limits of our experience of the Divine.

Along the apophatic path we leave behind all we thought we knew and understood of the Divine. Familiar thoughts, analogies, and images fall away, no longer able to pierce the thick cloud of darkness that hides God (Exod 20:21). In this darkness, even our images of God—Father, Mother, Shepherd, Wisdom, Comforter—are shattered, exposed as idols, since they falsely imply that we can describe an incomprehensible God. Usually described as originating with Pseudo-Dionysius, who wrote in about the sixth century in Syria, the apophatic approach marks the spiritual writings of *The Cloud of Unknowing*, an anonymous classic from the fourteenth century, and the works of John of the Cross.

The kataphatic approach to God emphasizes the similarity between God and creatures, and the human capacity to reach God through analogy and metaphor. The doctrines of creation and incarnation and of humans as made in the image of God assure us that we glimpse the divine radiance in all that is made. Nature, Scripture, and history each provide a window on the Divine. The lives and teachings of the sixteenth-century reformers Teresa of Avila and Ignatius of Loyola are examples of this path.

During certain periods in the history of spirituality, the apophatic and kataphatic paths have been ranked as higher and lower, more perfect and less perfect ways to God, usually with the apophatic being regarded as a more advanced spiritual state. However, a more complete perspective sees each as identifying a dimension of the individual and communal quest for the Holy. In most spiritual journeys the two are intricately intertwined—as when a fragile divine presence permeates the horrors of existence, or darkness and doubt shadow all creation's wonders. Historically, the great teachers of contemplation never lost sight of the fact that God leads us into communion in many ways, and methods of prayer simply open us to that encounter. When we turn to an ecological spirituality we find these two paths interwoven in our meetings with the Wisdom present throughout the cosmos. Sometimes contemplation of the universe evokes radical amazement. We stand in awe before the complex creation that evolved from the primordial explosion of a Big Bang fifteen billion years ago. The immensity and intricacy of the universe—the birth and death of stellar cycles, the textures of the planet Mars, the tiny specks of matter called interstellar dust—all this gives rise to wonder before the Divine Mystery.

But we may also encounter the silence of God in our cosmic narrative, finding no consolation, no comforting presence in the story of stars and planets. At every level, a veil of darkness hides the face of God. Encounters with floodwaters engulf us in a frightening and dangerous abyss. The old in nature decays and dies before we see the new forms of life to which it gives rise. A dark cloud of destruction hovers over nature. Such darkness now envelops lovers of trees in Colorado as they watch a pine-needle infestation reach epidemic proportions, fearing that their mature lodge pole pine forest will be killed within three to five years. As in all prayer of darkness, so cosmic contemplation asks us to renew our faith in the Spirit of God at work in the darkness, to trust the transfiguration we cannot see in our cosmic body.

Most apophatic approaches to prayer begin with a turn to the inner depths of the human person, to the God who dwells within. *The Cloud of Unknowing* describes a prayer that is imageless, silent, and vertical. This prayer reaches the depth of the personality, unifying it in radical detachment from all things. It strengthens our convictions and liberates us from desires and distractions, enabling us to seek the deepest truth at the heart of reality. In *Contemplative Prayer*, Thomas Merton asserted that if we descend into the depth of our own spirit and arrive at our center, we confront the inescapable fact that at the root of our existence we are in constant and immediate contact with God.

But interiority is not the same as individualism. Though Merton did not describe the contemplative experience in the language of quantum physics, it follows that this descent into the self takes us to that vast web of relationships where God dwells as its animating and sustaining presence. For the definition of the self has shifted with our changed worldview, and its depths are now understood as communal. In a universe in which relationships are essential and internal, there is no such thing as a separate, isolated individual. Prayer allows us to enter more fully into the cosmic dance. Quantum physics has taught us that nothing exists in itself, but only in relation to something else, which is in turn related to something else, and so on to the furthest reaches of the universe. When in the silence of contemplative prayer we encounter the God in whom we "live and move and have our being" (Acts 17:28), we meet all creation as well.

In shorter moments of centering throughout the day, we can deepen this awareness of the way contemplation links us with the entire cosmos. As an opening prayer for a retreat session, I have sometimes invited participants to choose another being from the universe—a fascinating planet, a beloved horse, a favorite rose, a single sparrow—and invite that creature to stand with them as they center. This joins them in silent praise before the Wisdom who made and cherishes us all. It concretizes the truth that all creatures are precious in God's sight.

SACRED READING OF
THE BOOK OF NATURE

The recovery of wisdom language to describe the Divine means that God is no longer viewed in isolation from nature. Further, this sapiential understanding of God's relationship to all creation situates individual prayer within a larger cosmic context.

Your steadfast love, O LORD, extends to the heavens,
your faithfulness to the clouds.
Your righteousness is like the mighty mountains,
your judgments are like the great deep;
you save humans and animals alike, O LORD.

(Ps 36:5–6)

An ancient contemplative practice offers a simple way to encounter God in nature. Usually known by its Latin name, *lectio divina*, literally, divine or sacred reading, this practice traditionally refers to prayer with a passage from Scripture or another sacred text, but it can also guide us in hearing God's word as revealed in what medievalists called the book of nature.

Lectio is not reading for information; it is essentially a practice through which the word of God shapes the heart and mind. Drawn from the Benedictine tradition, but meant for all, it consists of four progressive movements: Reading and hearing the Word of God (*lectio*), Meditation on the Word (*meditatio*), Opening our hearts to God in prayer (*oratio*), and Contemplation, or simply resting in God's love (*contemplatio*). This process deepens our prayer through slow and reverent listening to the Word, reflection on what has touched us, prayers that arise spontaneously from this pondering, and a silent presence to God. Its spiraling movement has been beautifully summarized by the French Benedictine monk Dom Marmion.

We read	(*Lectio*)
under the eye of God	(*Meditatio*)
until the heart is touched	(*Oratio*)
and leaps to flame	(*Contemplatio*)

This structure is not carved in stone, and it is possible to skip phases, move back and forth between movements, or enter at any point to which the Spirit takes us. The rhythm of the practice follows the pattern found in the deepening of a love relationship, where listening, reflection, and conversation give way to a presence that finally requires no words. At the conclusion of prayer, many find it helpful to take a word to carry with them through the day.

Some years before I knew anything about *lectio*, a retreat director suggested I spend my free time outdoors with an aspect of nature, asking it to teach me. I chose a colony of ants swarming across a road winding through the retreat center's farmland. First I simply sat and observed the ants' industry, which seemed to spring from some communal imperative. Then I noticed how vulnerable their tiny size and choice of location made them. From there I moved to prayer about the fragility of my own life and the human community itself. Then I simply sat in silence, taking in the summer sunshine and the beauty of my surroundings, giving thanks for these hours free of my usual hectic schedule and responsibilities.

Only much more recently did I discover the passage in the Book of Proverbs that invites us to observation of the natural world as a way to find wisdom.

Go to the ant, you lazybones;
consider its ways, and be wise.
Without having any chief

or officer or ruler,
it prepares its food in summer,
and gathers its sustenance in harvest.

(6:6–8)

Such time with nature becomes a form of *lectio*, and I suggest it to my retreatants during their own free hours. Some shape their responses creatively into poetry or dance.

An experience of listening to nature on a somewhat larger scale provided a powerful religious experience for the seventeenth-century Carmelite Brother Lawrence of the Resurrection. Wounded in the Thirty Years' War, he was forced into a period of inactivity and recovery that led to a conversion. It was winter, and looking at a tree outside his window that had lost all of its leaves, he began to reflect that the very same tree would be covered with leaves again, and then there would be blossoms and fruit where now there was nothing but bare branches. This revelation of God's power and presence never faded from his mind. He began a lifelong conversation with God that flowed indistinguishably through his prayer and work. It became known as the practice of the presence of God.

The book of nature offers countless passages for *lectio*: tumbleweed blowing across a stark desert terrain, Indian paintbrush pushing up through rocky mountain soil, a stand of poplars flaming into autumn red, orange, and yellow, a pod of orcas setting out to sea, the alternating arrival of storms and rainbows, the beauty of a cloud-covered firmament, or the seasons of sun and moon. *Lectio* often starts close to home, in our own neighborhoods, with a walk that expands how we listen to its landscape, trees, and seasons. Sacred reading can begin with looking, listening, observing, writing, sketching. At the end of prayer, the word one takes for the day might be a multicolored leaf, an agate from the seashore, a petal from a spring blossom, or a fresh vision of the night sky. Prayer with the book of nature often results in a changed presence to the rest of creation. As Chet Raymo comments in *Natural Prayers*, such mindfulness shows us how to watch "attentively for the light that burns at the center of every star, every cell, every living creature, every human heart."

Lectio divina is widely practiced as a form of communal prayer. It fits well when a small group wants to include prayer on a hike, a camping trip into the wilderness, or a bird-watching venture. The group selects a Word of nature for the prayer. A leader then guides them through its phases, starting first with a period of silence and then allowing time for those who wish to share briefly and simply, no more than a word or two, what they hear and see. A second period of silence follows, and then members of the group mention how the Word of nature touches their hearts. After the silence, those who wish speak any prayers that arise in their hearts. Members are free to share or not at any stage. At the end the group may include the way the prayer invites them to incorporate greater care of creation into their daily routines.

The spiritual classics, beginning with the New Testament, caution against judging the worth of prayer by what happens during it. Contemplation's long-term effect on everyday relationships and occupations constitutes the central criterion for assessing it. In the values by which we live and in the way we cherish ourselves, others, and the Earth, we find the fruits of prayer. This holds true as well of nature mysticism. Time spent with nature can have as its primary goal personal healing or an escape from the demands of human relationships. In this kind of mysticism, nature remains a commodity meant to serve our needs. In contrast, contemplation as understood in the Christian tradition gradually increases in us the life patterns that St. Paul tells us indicate the Spirit's presence: "love, joy, peace, patience, kindness, generosity, faithfulness, gentleness, and self-control" (Gal 5:22). An ecological spirituality interprets these fruits in terms of the Spirit's desire for the well-being of the entire Earth community. We know that we are living in union with Divine Wisdom when our lives are marked by the ecological virtues of gratitude, simplicity, restraint, frugality, and humility. This is not humility as self-negation and subservience, but an attitude in keeping with the term's derivation from *humus* or soil. It recognizes that we exist in solidarity with the rest of creation. Love, as the fruit of contemplative prayer, strengthens the web of relationships in the cosmos, transforming them in the pattern of Divine Wisdom.

CHAPTER 9

THE TRANSFORMATION OF DESIRE

But if we catch a glimpse of even the tiniest flash of this holy desire, we have found our way home.

—Wendy Farley

🌿 Teresa of Avila would be considered a fascinating woman in any era, but in sixteenth-century Spain, where women's voices were seldom heeded, her accomplishments stand out as even more remarkable. A mystic and religious reformer, she founded seventeen convents and wrote four books, securing a major place in Christian history as a doctor of the church. As impressive as her external works are, however, her spiritual evolution remains even more compelling. We first meet her as a charismatic and gregarious young woman, her energies scattered and her physical health precariously threatened by numerous illnesses. But at the age of thirty-nine, Teresa experiences a conversion. She glances one day at an image of Christ suffering on the cross, and is overcome with the contrast to her own spiritual mediocrity. She begs God to strengthen her.

What appears to be an instantaneous change of heart had been developing for a long time, however. In the years following her father's death in 1543, Teresa committed herself to a life of prayer, and through it she was gradually transformed from within by God's love. While often reluctant to remain faithful to her prayer times, she found herself emerging from them with greater serenity and delight. We might say that Teresa finds a life of true contentment, but not if that implies a satisfied and complacent existence. Rather, the contentment that fuels her later reform efforts comes from the transfiguration of her desires. Her strong will, quick mind, and ready wit, far from being diminished by her new focus, are amplified. Through prayer Teresa gained a new identity, a firm sense of authority to act on Christ's behalf in the world.

From Teresa's experience we learn that troublesome attachments are not broken by force, for they point to a deeper hunger. When that hunger is recognized, these entanglements no longer bind us with the same power. The witness of this mystic from centuries past suggests a way to meet our current global crisis, even though our situation might initially seem very different from the challenges she faced. The urgent need to reduce our pressure on the Earth's resources requires a similar exploration and transfiguration of the power of desire. In spite of the gospel summons to limit our material possessions and set our hearts on treasures that last, we have grown more, not less, attached to things, especially in the wealthier countries of the world. Teresa's conversion and passion for reform inspire us to look at our own scattered and restless longings and recognize how they are obscuring our larger desires. Then we will be ready to unmask the false promises of our consumer cravings.

A DEEPER HUNGER

As we know from trying to fathom the inner workings of our hearts, desires are complex and multilayered. Like the bindweed with which so many gardeners endlessly struggle, desire can be either a weed or a flower—an unwanted plant or its cousins, blue and white morning glories. When we try to pluck out bindweed, we find it has deep roots that can move great distances underground without being detected; despite our best efforts, it returns each morning and wraps its arms more tightly around other plants. So it is with desires. St. Augustine, who famously reminded us that our restless hearts will be at peace only in God, also remarks in his *Confessions* that the hairs of our head are far easier to count than our feelings and the movements of our heart. Several decades as a therapist and spiritual director have taught me that one of the most difficult questions for a person, especially a woman, to answer is: "What do I really want?" We seek a direction for ourselves and our world that is wise and loving, but it is not immediately clear which desires will be life-giving and which death-dealing.

The desires that consume us are perplexing manifestations of a deeper hunger. Inside our hearts and minds, we find a huge empty space, what we might call the God-space. We want desperately to fill it, and we believe that all we need is the right person, better sex, enough wealth, greater success, the latest car or fashions, and then all those gnawing feelings of emptiness will subside. A client once told me that when he reached unconsciously into his shirt pocket to pull out a cigarette and then started mindlessly drawing on it, he sensed he was really somehow reaching for God. This smoker is the image of all of us. Like him, we keep reaching mindlessly for *things*, when what we really want lies much deeper.

As twentieth-century theologian Karl Rahner reminds us, God is the *horizon*, the *beyond* which lies always at the far edge of the heart's reach for the good and the mind's search for the truth. The divine image is woven into our being, making our existence possible, but we live largely unaware of this deepest core. Everything we lay hold of both reveals and conceals, so communion remains partial. We drink in the grandeur of the cosmos, but find it filled with mysteries we cannot fathom—why was it made the way it is? What is human consciousness, and what is it all about? Everything we embrace holds a trace of the divine transcendence and yet falls short of it.

A deep restlessness, like an endlessly churning sea, keeps us ever aware of this gap between our present experience and our capacity for divinity: the tug of sorrow pulls at each joy, the shadow of loss hovers over all beauty, life's brevity haunts every accomplishment. When we reach for this or that thing, what we really want is Wisdom, happiness itself, mutual and abiding love. We, and the universe itself, were made for the fullness of God's presence, and no matter how good, how beautiful, or how true our experience turns out to be, we will continue to yearn for the *more* that is yet to be unveiled, for closure of the distance between the love we crave and the love we are now capable of giving and receiving. That means accepting as a painful fact of life a certain holy longing that never goes away, that is a taste of Wisdom and a call to greater communion, a preliminary experience of Sophia and an invitation to participate in the adventure that marks a self-creating universe.

In addition to the insufficiency of any finite good to fill our infinite hollow spaces, we face yet another obstacle to the sating of our hungers. Desire has been wounded, and evil reveals its darker strands. The history of sin distorts creaturely longings so that at birth each living being enters a universe shaped in part by abuse, violence, hatred, and greed. We are wounded in our worth, and dream of a healing and wholeness we never quite attain. Refusal to love fractures the relationships that constitute the web of life, poisoning the pool of connections from which all life emerges and preventing the Spirit's love from flowing freely. This wounding gives rise to unfulfilled desires stirring everywhere. It resounds in the cry of the Earth for release from human exploitation, in the passion for justice found across the globe, and in the longing of the majority of the Earth's peoples for basic aspects of human fulfillment—clean water, adequate food, the shelter of a home. We cannot isolate ourselves from these yearnings and remain immersed in our own wants and needs, for disturbances anywhere in creation invariably disturb our inner and outer world as well.

The British theologian and activist Mary C. Grey explores sacred longing on a global scale, drawing on her experience with Wells for India, which she and her husband helped found in 1987. The Greys created their nongovernmental organization in collaboration with a follower of Gandhi, and in response to a drought that killed sixty million animals, dried up wells, and sent Indian women farther into the desert in search of water. Grey notes that, in the Two-Thirds World, women must search daily for water, a precious resource now becoming ever more scarce. The United Nations Environmental Committee in May 2002 predicted that in 2032, 50 percent of the world will lack clean water; in Asia that shortage will reach 90 percent. Wells for India works specifically in three regions of Rajasthan, the second poorest state in India.

The longings of the women of Rajasthan are captured in the response of a landless woman to a workshop leader who asked if there was anything these women really yearned for: "I want to live in dignity, I do not want to be reduced to a state of helplessness where there is not respect for me as a human being—yes, that's what I want, I want to live in dignity." At the workshop, which was part of a women's empowerment program, village women were asked to imagine that some divine power had offered them ten wishes and they had one hour to prepare a wish list. At the end of the hour, the women named their desire for food, fuel, and a home; for equity among women and men, and all peoples; for justice and freedom from violence; for a world where children can attend school and enjoy their childhood; for a clean environment; for information from the world outside, and a say in the decisions that affect their lives. Leading the list was the desire for dignity—and running throughout it was the longing for water. Such divinely initiated desires can be heard around the globe. They represent a craving for justice and the basic necessities of life, standing in marked contrast with the wants and needs marketers create across that same global community.

MANUFACTURING DESIRE

In *One Perfect Day: The Selling of the American Wedding*, Rebecca Mead tells us that Americans spend $161 billion on weddings every year, an enormous consumer output fueled by a wedding industry designed to capitalize on our fantasies of happiness. "What," Mead asks the brides she interviews, "was the point of expending this much time, effort, imagination, and money? What was the wedding for?" The brides she talked with had not given much thought to this question about the larger purpose of the wedding. Rather, influenced by tradition and their own fantasies, they had come to see the event in terms of such items as floral arrangements, matching linens, and the scheduling of photographs. Nor were most of them aware that the white dress they selected so carefully for the occasion was created by Chinese bridal gown factory workers sleeping eight to a room and earning thirty cents an hour.

We know that the deeper wish of most brides centers not on the details of the wedding day, but on hopes for a joyous celebration with family and friends and a marriage of lasting friendship, intimacy, and happiness. Many look forward to raising children and creating a home and family. But Mead's exposure of the wedding industry reveals the power of marketing and commerce to create what we are supposed to want, while it masks our deeper desires.

Through her research, Mead provides one example of the many industries we hardly notice as they make large sums of money by altering and inventing our wants and needs. If we are out of touch with our true desires, we become easy prey for those eager to define them for us. Marketing, which relentlessly invades all areas of life, is double-edged. It tells us things we need to know about available products, but its larger purpose is to generate a desire for things we do not need. Advertisers link both personal worth and happiness to what we consume, so that fast cars equal admiration and the latest fashions promise acceptance and friendships. When the Center for a New American Dream, a group that advocates a less wasteful approach to life, polled Americans about their shopping habits, three-quarters responded: "Yes, we shop, but we don't really want to." Survey respondents believed that all the holiday gift giving simply increases children's already excessive materialism.

Consumerism thrives on the desire not only for something more, but for something other than what we already have. In other words, it turns our longing for transcendence into an agitated search for a more fulfilling product. This feeds the pervasive practice called *retail therapy*, shopping as a method of emotional coping. A client of mine whose mother had recently died after a long struggle with Alzheimer's disease told me that after the funeral she bought a new set of pots and pans for her kitchen and a chair for her living room, although she had no real need for any of these items. She was deeply puzzled that her response to her mother's death was this buying spree. She need not have been surprised. Desire motivates us, but it is a complex emotional state—in my client's case, a mixture of deep sadness at the loss of her mother, guilt over her inability to care for her during her final illness, anxiety about a future without a parent's presence, and anger at a God who could allow as devastating a disease as dementia. Rather than identifying the longings for love, safety, and forgiveness at the root of these feelings, she turned to action. We all do something similar—eat or drink too much, start a quarrel with a spouse or coworker, have a car accident, or come down with a cold—when our defenses against emotional pain are overwhelmed. And these unacknowledged or unexpressed emotions frequently fuel a trip to a shopping mall. Since this method of dealing with desire proves ineffective, it gets repeated again and again. Unchecked, such misplaced longings grow until, like potholes, they threaten to swallow us.

Discernment therefore holds a key place in any ecological spirituality, for it allows our deepest hungers to surface and shape our choices. But initial attempts to sort out our yearnings can feel like emptying a chest of drawers and confronting its odd assortment of contents. Understanding the motives for our actions requires a lifelong practice of sifting temptation and desire. This testing of the spirits has been a part of Christian spirituality from the time of the gospels, and is rooted in both a discerning community and a lifelong practice of prayer. In the New Testament, the discernment of spirits was seen as a charismatic gift intended for the faith of the entire community. As he names the gifts of the Spirit—wisdom, knowledge, healing, prophecy—Paul tells the Corinthians: "To each is given the manifestation of the Spirit for the common good" (1 Cor 12:7). Individuals as well as communities seek to discriminate among the spiritual states they experience in order to determine which are of God, and attention to a community's or an individual's unique experience takes place within a reading of the signs of the times. Surely in our era, these indicate widespread concern for the well-being of all species, and for the depth and equity of the relationships that pervade the universe.

The touchstone for discernment hearkens back to guidance offered in the biblical Book of Deuteronomy: "I have set before you life and death, blessings and curses. Choose life so that you and your descendants may live" (30:19). We make choices each day that contribute to fullness of life for the cosmos, or ultimately destroy the prospects of all creatures. Discernment helps us distinguish, in a variety of circumstances, which of these two paths we are taking.

Lifelong friendship with Sophia establishes the framework for discernment, for this ongoing prayer relationship gently shifts the affections. Time spent in her presence develops in us discerning hearts. For example, I may want to lower my carbon footprint in light of its heavy impact on the universe, but I also love to travel and, although aware of what it does to the atmosphere, may be reluctant to curtail my frequent plane trips. How do I weigh these conflicting movements? In his *Spiritual Exercises*, one of history's most influential teachers of discernment, Ignatius of Loyola, suggests that we see where a desire takes us. Does it strengthen or weaken connection with myself, others, the universe, and God? When I stay with my feelings, do they move me toward God and what is called consolation, or away from God and toward desolation? When Holy Wisdom moves us to a good choice, she works gently, aware of where we are and what we need to move forward. Ignatius compares the feeling of her prompting, in a person seeking God, to the way a drop of water penetrates a sponge. By contrast, a movement that is not of God feels to such a person like a drop of water falling on a rock. Ignatius's overarching spiritual vision, that we are to love God in all things and all things in God, grounds his counsels for discernment.

Ignatius suggests that at the beginning of any period of prayer, we ask God for what we want. Though we may have trouble doing this, the practice calls our attention to the fact that we experience attraction or aversion toward countless people, things, or ideas. It makes us aware that we have half-articulated desires, a vague sense that something—we know not what—is missing. But if over time we cut through these layers, we find that our deepest desire defines the most profound level of who we are. As we stumble along, led by the Spirit through our uncertainty, inadequacy, mistakes, and wrong turns, our desires are gradually over a lifetime purified and clarified.

Jesus tells us that life in the Spirit brings a peace that the world cannot give (John 14:25–27). Process thinkers would emphasize certain qualities of that peace. Since it results from an experience of the Spirit, it not only calms our turbulence and preserves the sources of our energy; it also bears a quality of movement and expansiveness. We sense that we have not escaped life's risks, but rather found in the Spirit the will and courage to meet them. In addition, the experience of this peace opens us to the larger communion of creation, to wider sympathies. Our choices are judged by the way we have enlarged our gifts and grown in the love of all beings. God wants fullness both for each individual and for the universe in which it dwells.

LONGING FOR SIMPLE THINGS

During the past few years a song that was first recorded by Louis Armstrong in the racially and politically tense period of the late 1960s has linked my extended family's encounters with times of intense sorrow and joy. The lyrics of that song, "What a Wonderful World," contain very simple images of red roses, blue skies, a baby's cry, the handshakes of friends, and the way the rainbow's colors are reflected in strangers' faces. The refrain, "And I say to myself, what a wonderful world," provides a frame for the ordinary joys mentioned. This song, in the Armstrong recording she loved, concluded the memorial service held for my sister after her death from a brain tumor. My brother-in-law discovered a version of the song, mixed with refrains from "Somewhere Over the Rainbow," while scuba diving in Hawaii. It brought him delight in the days before his sudden death. A few years later, my sister-in-law and her son chose to dance to "What a Wonderful World" at the son's wedding.

Perhaps the song proved so important to my family members, and has made it into the Hall of Fame, because it captures the human longing for the joy found in the simplest of things and for a community that embraces differences. It suggests that finding the *more* we seek exists in the moment we have right before us, if we enter into it deeply. Karl Rahner affirmed this sense that the particulars of life, like a cup of water offered a thirsty pilgrim, are vessels of grace. He believed that "the very commonness of everyday existence harbors the silent mystery of God." His words suggest a spiritual vision where we come to appreciate water as a precious drink and bread as the most satisfying of foods. In other words, we find the *more* that we seek by entering more deeply into the ordinary, rather than in reaching out for it in the accumulation of things.

Convinced that everyday things reveal universal mystery, Rahner insisted that we are all mystics. He applies this title, often associated exclusively with unreachable heights of God experience, to anyone who encounters grace in life's depths. Rahner finds a mystical dimension in all genuine human living—eating, drinking, sleeping, walking, sitting, and other daily activities. He regards the human person as an open question addressed to God. The answer to human longing comes as the unexpressed ambience that encircles, embraces, and upholds us. God is experienced in a quiet, silent, depth dimension to ordinary life. We also find God in the limits of existence: utter loneliness, forgiveness that goes unacknowledged or fails to make us feel good, radical fidelity to conscience even when we appear foolish, a tenacious hope in face of a seemingly hopeless death, and the taste of the difference between what we truly want from life and what it actually gives us.

If we, like the village women of India, were given an hour to express our desires, what would they be? When people I saw in counseling and spiritual direction could put words to their experiences, they shared the yearning of the Indian women—albeit from very different life contexts—for an end to violence, injustice, and abuse, and for the elimination of poverty and war around the globe. But they also named the healing of family relationships, forgiveness for their past failures, less harried lives and time for prayer and friendships, a sense that they were loved and accepted.

When we can articulate what it is we actually need and want, distinguishing those things that are essential and letting go of extra possessions, we are able to live deliberately and with contentment. This captures the kernel of recent cultural movements toward simple living—a life not so much of self-deprivation, but rather one of singleness of purpose. As characterized by those who have embraced voluntary simplicity, such a lifestyle requires the understanding and directing of our desires and energies, and the exercise of restraint in some areas in order to find greater abundance in others. Those who choose such simple living view it as a way to decrease the damage we are inflicting on the Earth, but also as a more fulfilling way of life and a path to lasting sources of contentment. It creates stronger community and aligns the use of money and time with deeper values. Paring down possessions—living in a place no larger than needed—opens time and energy for what matters. It frees us for art and music, the giving and receiving of care, play, and creativity.

The Sermon on the Mount provides a Christian formulation of this singleness of purpose. In the Beatitudes Jesus offers his disciples teachings that stand in sharp contrast to manufactured desires (Matt 5:1–12). They show us the values of God and how to pursue them in our own lives. These teachings make clear how longing is transfigured in the reign of God, how values are turned upside down so that mindless consumption is displaced by nonviolence, justice, compassion, and peacemaking. They tell us what to do with that surplus of restlessness that signals the limits to our present God experience. If you desire God, Jesus tells his disciples, learn to desire all that God desires, and direct your energy toward bringing it about. Pare down your life so that your longings will be distilled and refined by what will actually bring the joy you seek. Then you will, in the pattern of the Spirit, radiate love, alive to the divine energy at the heart of the universe.

The Beatitudes are familiar—perhaps so familiar that they have lost their power to challenge us. In addition, when we hear them all at once, we can feel overwhelmed by what is being asked of us. In order to deepen their meaning, we can turn to study and analysis. But another fruitful way of approaching the Beatitudes is to take each verse individually as a text for prayer, letting it provide the context for our discernment. Contemplation allows these verses to reach deep layers in the self and instill in us the paradoxical wisdom found in Jesus' sayings. Like a river that over time forges a canyon, or drops of water that eventually fill a container, a beatitude then alters our inner landscape. It also becomes the lens through which we view all of creation. We might begin to notice how mercy is displayed or withheld; the power of nonviolence or meekness to diffuse conflict; or the way being centered, pure of heart, opens us to creation's wonders. This paradox startles the imagination and sets in motion the conversion process. In this way it connects us in compassion and justice with those who suffer, and teaches us new ways of being with others and the Earth. This is one way in which the nurturing creativity of Sophia gradually educates our desires.

The new lens provided by the Beatitudes made for a surprising discovery one early December evening as I stopped at our local Quality Food Center to pick up some last-minute items for dinner. As I turned a corner and peered down the aisle in search of frozen corn, what I saw brought me to a halt. There, in front of the shelves of canned goods, a middle-aged man in suit and tie and a white-haired woman snug against the cold in her blue parka took lively steps together. Each had one arm wrapped around the other's waist. Over the loudspeaker a version of "Jingle Bell Rock" filled the store. Around them people moved with a frenzied need to get their shopping done as quickly as possible, visibly showing the stress that accompanies the holidays. In their midst a mother and son had interrupted their evening shopping to dance the grapevine to the Christmas song filtering through the store.

It struck me that Jesus would have loved this scene, enacted so near the celebration of his birth. Like the gospel parables, it offers a glimpse into what we would live for if we did not deplete our energies by acquiring and taking care of things, what it would be like if we were truly set free to love. A culture of *less*— already a way of life for the majority of peoples of the world— will need to be the pattern of life for all in the future. But a long Christian tradition tells us that we can find more of what we really want by having less of that which will never satisfy us. A certain kind of renunciation actually intensifies our joy. This paradox begins in Jesus' startling claim that those who lose their lives will find them, and in the promise contained in his death and resurrection. If we are to develop an ecological spirituality on behalf of our planet, we must embrace again this paradox that letting go leads to life.

An ancient Zen tale illustrates as well this truth about relinquishment and possession. One clear night, a monk sat in front of his hut on the mountainside, admiring the luminous glow of the full moon. As he gazed upward a thief crept, step by stone, up the mountain toward him. Arriving at the monk's hut, the thief demanded, "Give me all you own!"

The monk replied, "My hut is empty. I possess only these ragged clothes. Come and sit beside me. I am happy to share the night sky with you."

"Give me all you own!" demanded the thief again.

The monk removed his clothes and handed them to the thief. Bundling them under his arm, the thief crept, step by stone, down the mountain.

The monk sat shivering and naked in the moonlight, watching the thief disappear in the shadows. He sighed and thought, "What a poor man he is. I wish I could give him this beautiful moon!"

The effort to still desire with possessions and the counsel to seek an unencumbered life both beckon, like sparkling jewels dangled before our eyes. Which we choose will determine both true abundance and the survival of the planet.

CHAPTER 10

A NEW ASCETICISM

We live in such mystery it makes me wonder
who invented red-tag sales?

—David Craig

🌿 The restraint required to ensure our planet's future draws inspiration from the widely celebrated lover of nature, St. Francis of Assisi. Many know Francis through stories of his conversations with animals—Francis gently shaking the paw of the wolf of Gubbio or exhorting the birds to praise their Creator. Francis did indeed reverence creation, but he also lived a life of limits, choosing poverty in order to follow more closely the poor Christ of the gospel and withdrawing from the world for a time to live in prayer and penance as he served lepers and the sick. Renouncing possessions was of a piece with Francis's love of creation, and his asceticism never negated the material world or pronounced it evil.

In the *Testament* he dictated shortly before his death in October of 1226, Francis describes a defining religious experience. Raised in a privileged and comfortable lifestyle, he came face to face with human suffering in the person of a leper. A fastidious person, Francis found the poor and sick repulsive. Then one day while riding in the countryside he was moved to share his cloak with a leper and even to kiss the man's wasted face. That graced encounter overturned his values. What had previously seemed to him distasteful now brings an experience he calls *sweetness*.

The joyful simplicity that has proved so attractive an aspect of Francis's legacy was no naive optimism or mystical romanticism. The poet David Craig captures Francis's passion.

But how could he get his friends
to know what was real, and missing,
what demanded so much?

Francis integrated his gratitude for creation not only with a love of the poor, but also with a commitment to peace and an intense familiarity with the cross of Christ. These facets of his spiritual life are synthesized in the well-known poem he composed over the last years of his life, the "Canticle of Brother Sun." He added its concluding verses during his final days, while recovering from a preaching tour, in a hut outside the convent walls in San Damiano. Very ill and nearly blind, Francis knew that his brotherhood was roiled in bitter conflict over the interpretation of his rule. In this dark hour, he completed the hymn of praise that celebrates diversity, communion, and intimacy with Brother Sun, Sister Moon, Brother Wind, Sister Water, Brother Fire, Mother Earth—and, finally, Sister Death.

Francis's legacy encourages us to seek an asceticism that honors both the Earth and the poor, one based not in isolated self-mastery but in brotherhood and sisterhood, and one that promises a gospel joy not found in the pursuit of countless possessions. The following six guidelines suggest ways in which we might so redirect our attachments that the entire Earth community can thrive.

AN ECOLOGICAL SPIRITUALITY ROOTS ASCETICISM IN LOVE OF THE BODY AND CREATION

Like musty attic manuscripts, ascetic practices appear to have little relevance for our complex technological era. With growing awareness that our lifestyles must change if we are to save our planet, however, ascetical terms such as *restraint, sacrifice, limits,* and *discipline* have crept back into our common vocabulary. The term *asceticism* itself comes to us from the Greek *askesis,* the exercise or training that athletes undergo as they prepare to compete in games. Paul uses the concept that way when he applies it to the Christian life in his first letter to the Corinthians (9:24–27). He sees every Christian as an ascetic, running a race for an imperishable reward. Lest we be disqualified from that race, we should practice the self-control of athletes, and even be prepared to punish our bodies if necessary. Paul's metaphor evokes clusters of cyclists training for a triathlon, bodies bent over their handlebars as they endure pain and fatigue while straining toward the finish line. But Paul declares that all he does, including renouncing certain pleasures, is for the sake of the gospel and the blessings it brings. As a goal-oriented practice, asceticism makes room for a new set of values to replace the old.

In the decades since Paul urged on the Christian communities in Corinth, the practice of asceticism has taken a variety of forms—that of athletes such as Paul describes; of the early desert mothers and fathers; of scientists, artists, and caregivers; of single parents living in poverty, or drought-starved African farmers. In fact asceticism differs as much as the persons who undertake it and the historical contexts in which they live, making it a slippery notion to demarcate. Our most familiar Christian ascetic theories and practices emerge from the monastic tradition developed in fourth-century Egypt. We have inherited the experiences, both positive and negative, of these first monks of the desert, and of those who systematized their teachings. At its best, the tradition offers a rich array of insights and methods for developing an ecological asceticism, teaching us about craving and restraint, excess and simplicity. At its worst, it denigrates the material world and the body, puts a disproportionate focus on sexual renunciation, and extols suffering as a path to holiness. Its most respected teachers warn against such excess, however, and present asceticism as the work of the Spirit, transfiguring us into gospel freedom and love.

Asceticism can be either body-affirming or body-denying. In our time, it calls us to respect the finitude of our planet, treating it in such a way that all species can live well. For wealthy individuals and nations, this means relinquishing the culture of affluence, a shift that necessarily entails forms of self-denial. But this limit setting arises not from dualisms that set body and soul against one another, but from a love for all bodies and the body of the Earth. It rests on the realization that the planet's resources are at risk.

One widely embraced form of contemporary asceticism is the practice of fasting. Fasting, or abstaining in varying degrees from food and drink, is a discipline found in virtually every religion, and it stems from a variety of motives—repentance for sin, preparation for an important undertaking, supplication in time of need, protest against injustice. A practice both ancient and new, it offers an example of how asceticism must keep body and soul together and expand the meaning of body to encompass the entire planet. Linked with the meaning of the Eucharist as bread for the world, it expresses solidarity with the poor throughout the globe. In September of 2007, Pax Christi USA issued a call for a day of fasting as a way of raising awareness of the plight of our planet. They acknowledged how hard it will be to change our habits and lifestyles, and their fast sprang from love of the Earth and a conviction that we are called to act on behalf of the common good. What forms does fasting take when it fosters the common good? Such a fast might set limits to our careless use of water, recognizing what a scarce resource it is becoming worldwide. Disciplined care for water awakens us to the suffering of those who live in drought-stricken areas of the world such as Africa and the American Southeast. In the process, it revives appreciation for the blessings of water—its nourishing, cleansing, life-sustaining qualities.

Fasting in light of the common good might also consist in buying locally produced goods, foregoing sunflowers in November and raspberries in December if they must be shipped long distances to reach us. With this fast we support small farmers and learn where and how the food we eat was produced. These ways of fasting reconnect us with our physical selves, deepening rather than denying the bodily aspects of our existence. One imaginative group of neighbors extended this form of fasting into a community-building event, shopping together and then creating a meal each Sunday night from the seasonal produce they purchased at a local farmers' market.

As with all asceticism, illness or other considerations may indicate that fasting is not a good practice for us. It is especially important that women fast only if it honors the body and does not stem from a desire to master or punish it. Centuries of objectifying and idealizing their bodies have encouraged women's dissatisfaction with the way they look and contributed to the rise of eating disorders. Women—and men—who struggle with body image have the option of healing the planet through many spiritual disciplines unrelated to food. Since the car is one of the biggest sources of global warming, releasing twenty-five pounds of heat-trapping emissions for each gallon of gasoline it burns, car pooling, walking, bicycling, or taking public transit offer another form of fasting on behalf of the global community.

For those of us in countries dependent on cars, using other means of transportation takes notions of planetary communion out of the realm of abstraction and into the everyday. Public transportation inserts us into the physical universe. Like the majority of people on the globe we then have no metal box to shield us from bitter winds, heavy rain, or summer heat as we make our way to subway stations, wait at bus stops, cycle, or walk. Alternate modes of transportation are also more likely to carry the kind of mixed community Jesus came to save: the elderly, the racially mixed, the poor and homeless, those whose disabilities require canes or wheelchairs. Face to face, we find it more difficult to ignore one another's needs and aspirations. Nor can we deny serious societal issues such as the sexual harassment on public transportation that has led to a growing worldwide practice—already in place in India, Brazil, Mexico City, and Japan—of setting aside women-only spaces on trains, subways, and buses.

CHRISTIAN ASCETICISM READIES US FOR TRANSFIGURATION BY THE SPIRIT

Reflection on ecological asceticism often takes us to small issues that have larger consequences, such as the problem of plastic shopping bags that clutter streets and beaches and choke livestock and seabirds. China recently banned the thinnest plastic bags, joining several other countries such as South Africa, Ireland, Taiwan, and Bangladesh in the effort to control what they termed *white pollution*. A long-time resident of Kenya comments that plastic bags only recently arrived there. Fifteen years ago women used baskets for shopping, and he remembers buying fish and sweet potatoes wrapped in banana leaves, not plastic bags. Speed and convenience changed all that. The problem in Kenya is small compared to that of wealthier nations. It is estimated that we in the United States use one hundred billion plastic bags a year, throwaway bags that last nearly forever and take twelve million barrels of oil to produce.

When made aware of the problem, we determine to bring reusable bags for shopping, but our lives are too busy and chaotic. We forget the bags or find it too much of a bother to use them. Time itself proves to be a scarce resource that undermines our efforts. In contrast, there is the story of a woman in Portland, Oregon, a member of Leave No Plastic Behind, who brings a joyful, creative approach to recycling. She weaves plastic bags into stylish hats, using a skill she acquired in her native Nicaragua, where she and her friends braided kite and crepe paper into hats and purses during World War II. "I feel proud that I have a little imagination that I can lend," she says. "And I feel proud too that I'm helping in some small way with the environment."

When a Seattle family committed themselves to reducing their personal greenhouse gas emissions for one month, they thought it would mean many minor changes. It ended up turning their lives upside down, as they realized how hard it is to change habits and begin switching off lights, unplugging electronics, driving less, and living in a cooler house. Where can we find the will to protect our planet when the daily care of self and family and preoccupation with immediate concerns absorb our time and energy? The apostle Paul named this dilemma precisely in his letter to the Romans: "For I do not do the good I want, but the evil I do not want is what I do" (7:19). Like Paul, we struggle to do the good—to reduce our negative impact on nature—and find to our dismay that we fail to fulfill our aspirations to live a simpler life. In his letter to the Galatians, Paul tells us that release from shortsighted goals comes as a gift of the Spirit. When we open to her, our consciousness is gradually transformed, and we discover ways to make changes, small though they may seem at first.

The most complete understanding of the Spirit's transfiguration embraces the reality of death and resurrection. Notions of sacrifice and self-denial evoke the cross and require us to be clear about its meaning in Christian life. Jesus asks his disciples to deny themselves and take up the cross if they want to follow him. He also tells us that this relinquishment is actually the way we will find what we are seeking: "For those who want to save their life will lose it, and those who lose their life for my sake will find it" (Matt 16:25).

Understanding its place in Jesus' life helps us interpret the cross in our own experience. Jesus did not choose suffering for its own sake. The gospels show clearly that he loved life and enjoyed its fundamental goodness. Close friends offered him support and companionship. He ate and drank with them in celebration and anticipation. But a larger goal centered his life—the elimination of suffering and hatred, of all that keeps human beings from God. In other words, he wanted us to live in right relationship with one another and with the rest of the universe. In pursuit of that love and justice, he was willing to walk the path of suffering, even to death, if necessary. This provides a model of asceticism where suffering and the cross are not a denial of the good creation, not ends in themselves, but the outcome of seeking God's reign.

Asceticism is voluntary. It must not be used as a justification for glorifying suffering or as a way of encouraging victims of abuse and violence to endure pain and the violation of their rights. The cross and resurrection are one with Jesus' struggle against injustice and his solidarity with all those who seek life. Crucifixions witness to the power of evil in the world, and to the price exacted of those who enter fully into Jesus' mission to bring an end to that evil. It was not sacrifice that Jesus sought, but reciprocal and mutual relationships, love free of inequality. Seen in this way, the cross lies at the heart of an ecological faith. For we are called to right the wrong relationships that exist among all species on our planet—to protest the injustices that strangle the very goodness God intended for the universe.

ASCETIC PRACTICES ARE NOT ENDS IN THEMSELVES, BUT MEANS TO THE REIGN OF GOD

In one of her last speeches before her death, the social critic Susan Sontag mourned the spread of American consumer values around the world, especially the way they promote a global culture of individual gratification and materialism. She believed this coarsens sensibilities and thwarts peoples' capacity for goodness. What Americans often export is the tantalizing vision of consumption as the way to happiness. Sontag warns of the dangers this presents, as well, to artists and thinkers. No true culture exists, she insists, without altruism and regard for others. Her point seems punctuated by billboards in India advertising new cars with slogans such as, "Your American relatives are not the only ones who can enjoy the good life."

We might extend Sontag's observation by noting that discipline is essential to all love and creativity; we need it throughout our lives. In order to choose each day to love the world again, to let hope and gratitude shape our actions, we must rein in the impulse to give up on a human enterprise beset by violence and seemingly intractable problems. So also, developing a life of prayer requires that we come back to it faithfully even when God seems distant or absent and when we have lost the taste for such disciplined waiting. And anyone who has cared for a feverish child or a spouse with cancer knows how much asceticism human love requires, how in practicing it we forego many pleasures, often even sleep and food.

In her analysis of the history of asceticism, theologian Margaret Miles points out that there is much that is new in traditional asceticism, and much that is old in our efforts to give it a fresh face. She looks at four historical examples—the desert mothers and fathers, early monasticism, Augustine, and Ignatius of Loyola—arguing that, in spite of the excesses and distortions that often arose, each era found spiritual disciplines life-enhancing. She believes the immediate goals of these ascetic traditions are applicable today: self-understanding, movement beyond deadening habits and addictions, the intensifying and focusing of energies, changing cultural conditioning, and expanding awareness. These historic Christians, she notes, wanted to stay oriented to the Source of life, but they believed that they could not do this by insight alone. They needed spiritual practices that addressed the whole human being, body and soul.

The women and men who fled to the Egyptian desert in the fourth and fifth centuries were seeking self-knowledge as a necessary step on the way to the reign of God. They saw spiritual disciplines as ways of exploring all the dimensions of the human psyche. The soul, they believed, is made in the divine image; but only when the psyche is understood, when we see our faces as if in a glass, does it become a clear image of the Divine. Because of their emphasis on controlling the irrational urges that cloud and disturb the interior life, their approach has sometimes been called therapeutic asceticism. Through solitude and simplicity they sought to refocus the many concerns clamoring for attention, turning to a calmer focus on God and neighbor.

Such naming and redirecting of our deeper cravings remains a valuable function of the spiritual disciplines. We often eat or shop our emotions, harming our own bodies and the Earth's body in the process. Many of my therapy clients tell of consuming a quart of ice cream after a distressing phone call, or of buying a new dress to compensate for the emptiness of a marriage. The prayer and discernment necessary to change these patterns function on behalf of the planet. When we become transformed, we inevitably transform the world around us. This basic principle of change, long emphasized in the spiritual life, holds even more force in a worldview that recognizes intrinsic relations as the way the universe operates.

ASCETIC PRACTICES FREE US FOR LOVE AND WORK

Like the frame that gives a painting definition, limits allow us to live with intentionality. The New Testament calls this way of life purity of heart, a term that can mistakenly be applied primarily to the realm of sexuality. "Blessed are the pure in heart," Jesus tells us, "for they shall see God" (Matt 5:8). When we set our sights on what really matters and direct them to the source of life, we find a joy that otherwise eludes us. The Carmelite tradition notes that asceticism is aimed at what John of the Cross calls freedom of the heart for God. Purity of heart opens a space for God's love to enter.

146

Clare of Assisi, the thirteenth-century foundress of the Poor Clares, understood clearly how a certain detachment gives rise to freedom. She was convinced that we cannot direct our hearts and minds to anything when they are already absorbed with something else. Clare believed that letting go of possessions allowed her to turn her attention, love, and will wherever she chose to direct them. Spiritual disciplines free us from a preoccupation with things; when these attachments are released, God can fill up all those spaces. We instinctively trust the witness of those who embrace a certain personal renunciation in the service of others, while regarding with suspicion religious figures whose lives seem driven by wealth, fame, and power.

The kind of emptying out that Clare describes as part of the search for the Holy occurs often in a spiritual journey. The tradition calls it purgation, and we recognize it in every transition that takes us to a new level of love. Purgation and union, at times described as a sequence, actually alternate throughout a lifetime, since purgation creates the empty space into which love may enter. My mother practiced this kind of emptying out in the final stages of her life. In the last years before her death, she began giving away her personal possessions. To a son or daughter who visited she would present a jewelry box and beads, a framed picture of a snowy village, or a ceramic angel plaque, each carefully wrapped in whatever paper she had on hand. My mother was never a wealthy woman, and most of what she owned had originally come as a gift from one of her children. My brother once remarked that she loved to receive presents so that she would have something to give. But her late-life gift giving was more than an expression of her bigheartedness. By this final simplifying she intended to reduce clutter and turn her attention to the essentials: family and friends, gratitude for her blessings, and the tulips and cedars outside her apartment window. Her divesting herself of belongings exemplified the gospel admonition to seek wealth that does not wear out and riches that moths cannot destroy (Luke 12:33).

In his introduction to *The Wisdom of the Desert*, Thomas Merton describes the ascetic life as the way to free ourselves from a false and socially constructed self in order to find our true self in Christ. In other words, we are in the gospel realm of dying to self so that we can be reborn to a new self. Only the ascetic becomes inwardly free to become what we are meant to be and finds the self beyond the trappings imposed on us. The notion of the true and false self runs through Merton's writings and finds contemporary meaning in the struggle to counter consumerism.

Much in the Western developed nations defines us in terms of what we consume. Accumulating possessions promises to confer value on us and bring us salvation. Buying and acquiring become patriotism, a way to preserve the economy and the nation. Refusing to be thus defined offers a contemporary way of doing what ascetics have done throughout history—fleeing the world. This withdrawal consists in refusing to conform to certain cultural imperatives. In keeping with what Jesus meant by the world, we turn from the life-denying forces that foster their own interests by encouraging frenetic consumption. Such asceticism helps us resist those who—by selling us cigarettes, hamburgers, or video games—determine our habits and identity.

Distancing from deadening social patterns enables us to discern healthier paths of recreation, work, and consumption. Historically it has often been those who first sought individual conversion who made the greatest positive difference to their culture. When St. Benedict withdrew to a cave near Subiaco, his intention was to save his own soul, not Western civilization. But he did make a major long-term contribution to that culture. All asceticism implies some withdrawal from dominant cultural patterns in order to embrace a larger truth.

COMMUNITY PROVIDES BALANCE AND SUPPORT FOR ASCETICISM

In *Sinners Welcome*, her fourth book of poetry, Mary Karr tells how she grudgingly turned to prayer as a last-ditch effort to stem the tide of her alcoholism. Determined to care for her baby son, she got down on her knees morning and night. To her surprise, she eventually stopped drinking. Karr began to see that the cynicism she considered a realistic appraisal of life was a projection of her own self-pity.

When her six-year-old son, Dev, suggested that they start looking in churches to see if God is there, she was ready. Eventually this led Karr, a lifelong agnostic, to become an unlikely convert to Catholicism. She writes with enthusiasm of how the carnal nature of the church's rituals—the motion of physically standing, sitting, and kneeling with others during the Mass, the act of lighting candles and talking to statues—stilled her mind and linked her with others. This sense of being part of a community persisted even outside of church.

Asceticism finds its moorings in such incarnational gatherings. Vigils, pilgrimages, attendance at services—these provide the communal setting for reviving a sense of what matters. Community moderates and directs our efforts, helping us avoid the distortions that have sometimes plagued ascetics in the past. It also helps with consistency. Spiritual practices such as prayer require patience and persistence. We grow less discouraged when we pursue them in a community context. In community we also reinforce one another's efforts to use and reuse materials, to find alternate sources of energy, to preserve the world's forests.

A community's larger vision of the world keeps us aware that we share in the redemption of every person, plant, animal, and cell of the fragile universe. Together we seek ways to live simply and with less so that monarch butterflies can continue to migrate and island peoples throughout the globe will not lose their homes to rising seas. Excess produces boredom and restlessness, but true celebration sustains and strengthens.

BOTH RENUNCIATION AND CELEBRATION CHARACTERIZE THE RHYTHM OF CHRISTIAN EXISTENCE

Recently a group of grade school friends and I were reminiscing about how we understood Lenten penances while growing up. We saved our candy during the week (I deposited mine in a used cigar box), and then ate it on Sunday or at the end of Lent. Giving it up permanently would not have occurred to us. We also attempted to kneel during Benediction of the Blessed Sacrament without letting our arms touch the pew. We were inspired by saints such as the fourth- to fifth-century hermit, Simeon Stylites, who spent thirty-seven years on a small platform at the top of a pillar, seeking there the solitude that eluded him elsewhere. In our eagerness to imitate the saints, we managed to make self-discipline an end in itself. As we advanced in age and wisdom, we realized that a focus on ascetic practices in themselves proves to be enervating and distracting.

What we did learn well from our early experiences, however, was the rhythm of renunciation and celebration that characterizes the liturgical year. Having spent Lent in the stark terrain of the desert, we were ready for the lush smell of Easter lilies and the exultant ring of alleluias, ready to ritualize the joy that Easter's celebration evoked. Among the things I remember most vividly from my Roman Catholic childhood are its feasts and rituals. They introduced me to the rhythm of the seasons, made clear what was expected of me, and provided an opportunity to express feelings of longing, hope, guilt, and gratitude. I recall very little of the doctrine I must have learned during those years, but I do retain memories of the expectation engendered in me as we lit the Advent wreath, and the solemnity of having ashes placed on my forehead on Ash Wednesday. A high point of the school year was crowning a statue of Mary amid the strong fragrance of May lilacs. In all these ways I learned that ascetic practice has its celebrative counterpart—silence gives way to song, fasting issues in dancing, and solitude finds its fullness in communal worship.

Hispanic Christians have much to teach us about celebration and fiesta. Although their worship takes numerous and diverse forms, it is characterized by a sensuous flavor—vivid colors, abundant flowers, numerous candles, the sounds of music, the rhythm of movement, and cries of longing or joy. All this provides a feast for the eyes and the senses, a celebration that involves the whole body. In worship, the participants are gathered "to celebrate the fiesta of God and God's people." Family life is filled with *flor y canto*, flower and song, and family is not a tightly defined and exclusive group, but an extended family of those related in multiple ways, whose limits are never tightly defined. Good Friday processions and Christmas posadas, festivals in honor of Our Lady of Guadalupe—all these express belief in a God who knows both the struggles and the joys of existence. Such celebration belongs intrinsically to an asceticism that honors Earth and all bodies. It answers our longing to feel, to belong, and to draw close to the Creator found in all creation.

CHAPTER 11

IN A DARK TIME
WE BEGIN TO SEE

The greatest figures of prophecy and sanctity step forth
from the darkest night.

—Edith Stein

One afternoon several years ago I lost my way in the sand
dunes along the Oregon coast. I had stopped in Florence,
Oregon, to explore its dunes and suddenly, surrounded by endless grainy horizons, all sense of direction vanished. With each
step my feet sank deeper into the blowing sand and I began to
panic. Would I keep circling forever, falling further into an
abyss? Voices finally echoed in the distance and, following them
to their source, I discovered a parallel path to the sea just at the
edge of the dunes.

As we enter the twenty-first century many fear that humanity is in fact circling an abyss, that we have lost our way and must heed the voices that show us a new direction. Indications of our disorientation are clear. Billionaires increase in number even as millions of people from Detroit to Bangladesh go to bed hungry each night. The twentieth century has left a legacy of widespread violence, witnessing the most wars of any comparable period in history. Climate change, if continued unchecked, will lead by the middle of this century to the extinction of a quarter of the planet's animal and plant species, to melting glaciers and rising seas. One young post-Katrina volunteer in New Orleans brings immediacy to these issues in a comment on his blog: "It can be an emotional and meditative process, scraping out the debris of someone's broken life, what feels like the postapocalyptic fallout of a failing empire."

These realities constitute what might be called a cultural dark night of the soul, and the spiritual traditions that probe that darkness offer insight and hope for the situation in which we find ourselves. They show us the nature of the changes we must undergo in order to experience again the well-being God desires for all creatures. From these traditions we learn how to be and to love during dark times, when forms of knowledge and trusted systems no longer work the way we once thought they did. In the Book of Genesis the darkness that covers the face of the deep is the matrix from which the Spirit of God brings forth all creation. We trust that this Creator Spirit will also illumine our current darkness and call us forth to life.

NOTHING WORKS THE WAY IT ONCE DID

In the year 1577 powerful opponents within the Carmelites arrested their fellow friar Juan de Yepes in Toledo, Spain, and threw him into a six-by-ten-foot prison cell. Their actions were fueled by anger at his rebellion against their faction of the order, as well as by suspicions about his relationship with the Carmelite reformer Teresa of Avila. This friar, known to us by the name he took in religious life, John of the Cross, spent nine months in a dank and windowless cell whose only light came from an opening in the wall a few inches wide near the ceiling. Denied books and adequate food, he suffered as well from extremes of heat and cold and from regular beatings. But even before his imprisonment, John had known deprivation. Raised in grinding poverty, he later encountered grim human misery while working as a nurse in a hospital that specialized in ulcers and contagious diseases, including syphilis, one of the scourges of his time.

These experiences seem unlikely soil for soaring spiritual poetry and writings filled with joy and delight. Yet during his confinement in his Toledo prison cell, John composed in his mind the poetry and treatises he later put on paper as *The Dark Night* and *The Ascent of Mount Carmel*. A profound Christian exploration of loss and transformation, the concept of the dark night entered spiritual literature primarily through his works, and it continues to resonate beyond the borders of mystic and monastic life. John's writings contain psychological and theological perspectives on affliction, loneliness, and despair, and furnish a paradigm for understanding the dark nights of personal and cultural existence.

An awareness of limits characterizes the dark night experience. When John of the Cross developed this metaphor, he was thinking primarily of the life of prayer, describing those points when our usual approaches to God no longer work. Previously comforting paths of prayer—the repetition of sacred words, meditation on favorite biblical passages—become impossible, and we find ourselves deadlocked. John says, "Everything seems to be functioning in reverse." God, like misplaced keys, is nowhere to be found. Simply trying harder only makes things worse. Failing to find a way out, we are tempted to give up. The systems and practices on which we have relied now give way. In fact, our very identity comes under siege, and John tells us that it is as if we are imprisoned in a dungeon unable to move because we are bound hand and foot and cannot see or feel any earthly or heavenly comfort.

What can we do? When this happens, John advises us to stay in loving and peaceful attentiveness to the Divine, though this proves difficult when God has apparently disappeared from the horizon. In personal as well as global dark nights, a divine presence is quietly and unceasingly bringing about something new beneath this veil of mystery. This is the paradox—absence is in fact a kind of presence. We cannot see or feel this; we know it only by faith and hope. As we are gradually purged of old ways of loving, a deeper kind of love is being born, but it is hard to believe in this transformation when we are accustomed to receiving love in another more familiar way. In *The Spiritual Canticle*, John prays: "Transform me into the beauty of Divine Sophia and make me resemble the one who is the Word, the Son of God." It is important to remember that it is *in* the very experience of darkness that transformation is taking place. If we could see the underside, we would realize that we are gradually being readied for a new vision and experience. God contradicts our plans and expectations in order to fulfill our desires and freedom at a much deeper level.

The prayer of Jesus in the Garden of Gethsemane, which was a favorite biblical passage of Teresa of Avila, provides the paradigm for prayer in such times. As Jesus' ministry collapses all around him and he contemplates the bleak path ahead, he cries out in anguish, "My Father, if this cannot pass unless I drink it, your will be done" (Matt 26:42). Jesus experiences here the dark night, the emptying that allows God's love to flow unimpeded into the human heart. The darkness does not derail his prophetic mission. Rather, it opens out into resurrection.

When plunged into unfamiliar darkness, we at first bump into objects and grope to find our way. Eventually we become accustomed to the darkness and begin to see. Although the negative way takes us into darkness, its purpose is ultimately to illumine. The night becomes the realm of revelation and a prelude to new vision. First, however, we face the limits of our knowledge, speech, and prayer.

DARK LOVING

Even as we celebrate the beauty of creation and the cosmos, we feel alone at times in our sense of responsibility for its future, insignificant in light of its intricate processes. Sophia seems more absent than present in polluted seas and drought-stricken landscapes, violent human conflicts and personal suffering. But the negative way, as it manifests itself in both prayer and speech about God, does not depend on uplifting thoughts and feelings. It rests on the primacy of love. Whether God is silent or responsive, what matters is the pattern of our existence.

Each of our relationships—marriages, friendships, religious and political commitments—comes up against an impasse at some point. Perhaps we realize that we no longer feel the same kind of affection we once had for a spouse. Do we still love this person? we wonder. Or a friend disappoints us in a time of need, and the whole relationship is thrown into doubt. Our churches and political systems reveal their deeply flawed nature, plunging us into distrust and disillusionment. In these seasons of transition familiar moorings slip away as we undertake a voyage toward deeper freedom and love.

Our ordinary forms of dark loving are illumined in a striking way by the life of one of the most beloved figures of the twentieth century, Mother Teresa of Calcutta. Key events in her spiritual narrative begin on September 10, 1946, as a train speeds from Calcutta carrying her as a young nun to a retreat house in Darjeeling, India. During this trip, the woman who would later be revered throughout the world as Mother Teresa of Jesus first realized that she was being called to radical service to India's poorest people. In private letters to her spiritual director, she described a conversation on that train journey in which Jesus tells her of his desire to have Indian nuns work with the poor, the sick, and the dying, as well as with little children. "Would thou not help?" Jesus asks. "How can I?" Mother Teresa replies. Just thirty-six, and happy with her life as a missionary sister of Our Lady of Loreto teaching in a convent school in Calcutta, Teresa envisioned ridicule and failure if she said yes to this new summons. She recoiled from the loneliness and deprivation she feared would overtake her if she lodged among the destitute and dying on the streets of India.

We know the public results of Mother Teresa's decision to don a rough sari, live on the meager diet of the poor, and soothe the agonies of the desperately ill, but we have assumed that she was sustained in her daily rounds of care by a palpable sense of Christ's presence. Now we know that was not the case. During the investigation of Mother Teresa's life that preceded her beatification in Rome on October 19, 2003, the letters she sent to her spiritual directors became public, and parts of them have been published in *Mother Teresa: Come Be My Light*. They reveal that while she experienced a deep sense of union with Christ throughout 1946 and 1947, this spiritual consolation ended soon after she started her work on the streets. From then until her death in 1997, Mother Teresa experienced only spiritual darkness. She tells her spiritual directors that God feels absent and her sufferings seem to count for nothing. She can find no words, she says, to describe adequately the depths of this darkness. In 1959 she writes: "In my soul I feel just that terrible pain of loss, of God not wanting me—of God not being God—of God not existing."

So we learn, contrary to our assumptions, that when Mother Teresa wiped the sores of the lepers and washed the feverish bodies of the dying, she did so out of a dark faith and a dark love. Her relationship with God was sustained, not through a felt presence of the Divine or some kind of spiritual ecstasy, but by daily fidelity to the smallest acts of love. She saw this darkness as her Gethsemane, her own sharing in the sense of abandonment that Jesus suffered as he stared death in the face in the garden and on the cross, crying out to a silent and absent God.

Many prophets, saints, and public figures of faith have experienced spiritual darkness and doubt. This includes Mother Teresa's own namesake, Thérèse of Lieseux, who died in spiritual dryness, wondering if anything at all awaited her after death. Yet the length and unrelenting nature of Mother Teresa's experience, spanning her entire Calcutta ministry, seems without parallel. It is nonetheless characterized by the mark of a genuine dark night—her continued faithfulness to work and prayer. In time she began to see how her experience enabled her to identify not only with Jesus, but also with the poor to whom she ministered. She said she hoped to enter the *dark holes* these people experienced.

In Mother Teresa's life we encounter in the strongest possible terms the paradox of how God can be most present when most absent, how a person can be a vessel of light while feeling nothing but darkness within. The contemporary ideal of solidarity with the poor and oppressed takes on new depth and concreteness in her continued commitment to serve the poor of the Calcutta slums in spite of her own lack of spiritual consolation. She remarked in

1962 that if she were to be declared a saint, she would be a saint of *darkness*. And, in fact, we may need her witness to the power of dark loving as much as, or more than, we required the global influence she exercised as an admired religious leader.

DARKNESS AND A RELATIONAL GOD

Themes of darkness and illumination take new shape in a cosmos in which relatedness is understood to be the primary reality. In the universe as we now know it— composed of interwoven strands that could not exist without one another—communion is foundational to all life. How might we understand aspects of our cultural dark night in such a collectively constituted universe? Writers from two different traditions offer their interpretations.

Theological reflection on the Holocaust represents one attempt to deal with the question of how we can speak of the divine presence and absence in view of the brutal genocides of our century. Decades of reflection have not resolved the complex and troubling question of reconciling such suffering with a good and loving Creator. Nonetheless, each generation offers its tentative insights.

Many Jewish theologians conclude that God was hidden during the Holocaust, either shrouded in mystery or deferring to human action. But in *The Female Face of God in Auschwitz*, the British theologian Melissa Raphael offers an alternative interpretation of the divine absence. Raphael draws on the published testimonies of women who were imprisoned at Auschwitz-Birkenau to argue that the relationships of care between women in the death camps invited the Divine into this place of immense evil where God was apparently absent and indifferent. She changes the customary question, *Where* was God in Auschwitz? to *Who* was God in Auschwitz?

Raphael does not minimize Nazi savagery. But she believes that women's experience in the death camps tells us something about how God was present but concealed there. She turns to the traditional religious image of the Shekhinah, the female divine presence that accompanies Israel into exile. This is not a God who displays power over others, but a God who suffers with the suffering. The Shekhinah, which literally means *dwelling*, refers in classic rabbinic literature to God's presence in the world. In that literature, Shekhinah is feminine and synonymous with God. *She-Who-Dwells-Among-Us* accompanies Israel into her deepest exile. God's face, as that of the exiled Shekhinah, is revealed in Auschwitz in the female face turned to the other in compassion.

Women's experience in the death camps was filled with filth—inadequate sanitation, grimy clothing, lice, fleas. Their attempts to wash themselves and others and their willingness to see, touch, and cover the bodies of the suffering reveal the refracted divine image. These acts of purification uphold the covenantal obligations of the victims to God and to one another. Raphael proposes that "where women in Auschwitz, each in God's image, turn (in whatever sense) to face the other, they refracted God's face or presence into the world from the light of their own. Compassion was transfigurative." In the Holocaust God was present as women extended an arm to steady another, secretly handed someone a piece of bread as they passed, covered a shivering woman with a shawl, or simply offered a comforting presence. By nurturing each other, women momentarily transformed the darkness of Auschwitz.

Extending the meaning of redemption in Auschwitz, Raphael draws on Jewish mystical traditions, especially the notion of *tikkun olam* or repair of the universe. She speaks truthfully of the brokenness as well as the connectedness of Jewish women's relationships during the Holocaust, and finds an analogy for *tikkun*, the mending of an unraveled world, in women's skills of darning, patching, knitting, and the bandaging of wounds. In a world that is an interconnected whole, the violation or the reconsecration of anyone is that of all. When mothers covered their daughters by sewing together rags and pieces of cloth, or knit a wrap to keep another warm, their love stopped the universe from unraveling and anticipated the renewal of its fabric.

This theme of the redemptive power of relationships occurs in the fictional exploration of another kind of contemporary darkness—the threat of global disaster. Although the novelist Cormac McCarthy is not writing explicitly from within the classical dark night tradition, his novel *The Road* enables us vividly to contemplate experiences found in that literature and to extend their meaning beyond the interior life to our current cultural context. In dark nights both personal and cultural, we are first freed from what impedes God's love; a kind of emptiness prepares the way for the reception of light. Spiritual literature names these movements purgation and illumination and usually describes them as sequential—even hierarchical—stages of prayer. But they often occur simultaneously.

A stark purgation pervades McCarthy's fictional eschatology, *The Road*. In this eloquent work, for which he was awarded the Pulitzer Prize, McCarthy portrays, in bleak and unrelenting detail, a postapocalyptic America. In the novel, an unnamed father and son journey across a land enveloped in cold, wet darkness. Color, with the exception of fire and blood, now inhabits only memory or dream. All is gray, and the river water flows black. Ash clings to everything in a devastated landscape where vegetation has perished, and the pair must forage for every bite of food and drink of water. Vigilantes roam the land, and trust between human beings evaporates in the struggle for survival. We are never told exactly what catastrophe devastated the land, only that at 1:17 the clocks stopped, accompanied by a long shear of light and several low concussions, as a dull rose glow appeared in the window's glass.

Yet this story of nearly total negation, set against a background devoid of almost everything that characterizes human life in the developed world, becomes a tale of love between father and son and a fragile kind of redemption. The cataclysmic purgation brings new vision, revealing the insignificance of what once was thought highly important—fancy electronics, gold Krugerrands. They find an old newspaper, and the father comments on "The curious news. The quaint concerns."

What remains of unsurpassing value is relationship, the bond between father and son and the moving tenderness between them. The son is the father's sole reason to go on living: "He said: If he is not the word of God God never spoke." What breaks the father's heart is the realization that he will eventually send his son to fend for himself in a ruined world. Yet moments of ecstasy and mystery erupt in this grim world: The father suddenly sees his son as a "chalice, good to house a god" and "glowing in that waste like a tabernacle." In such ways Cormac's parable suggests a radiance beyond the horror in which it imaginatively steeps us.

Story and ritual survive in the darkness. As if to provide a reason to struggle on, the father tells his son that they are "carrying the fire." The nature of this fire is never specified, but the boy takes from it the promise that someday life will be different, that sunlight and green will return. Because they are carrying the fire through a world destroyed by fire, father and son embody a fearless wisdom, a kind of faith before the utter hopelessness that surrounds them.

Toward the end of the novel, wracked by an increasingly ominous cough, the father dies. After three days of grieving, the boy walks out to the road again, where he meets a couple who take him into their care.

The woman when she saw him put her arms around him and held him. Oh, she said, I am so glad to see you. She would talk to him sometimes about God. He tried to talk to God but the best thing was to talk to his father and he did talk to him and he didnt forget. The woman said that was all right. She said that the breath of God was his breath yet though it pass from man to man through all of time.

The boy must struggle on and somehow contribute to the world's rebirth. In the end, *The Road* strikes an ambiguous note of new life.

PRAYING IN THE DARK

In the closing sections of *The Road*, the boy raises the question of how he is to pray in such times. That question of prayer is also where our reflections on the dark night ultimately take us. Like the boy, we discover that there are different kinds of darkness and different ways of praying in their midst.

The Cloud of Unknowing describes one such path. Though we cannot comprehend God with our knowledge, we can each in our own way grasp God through love. The author teaches us how to dwell in such a cloud of unknowing. We are to relinquish concepts and images until, left with only love, we feel and see God in this life. This dark love illumines reality, but it also purges and cleanses; it shows us our sins but also heals them. How can we bear to dwell in this unknowing? The author of *The Cloud* counsels us to rely for our grounding on a simple word, one that has meaning to us: "so to have a better grasp of it, take just a little word, of one syllable rather than two, for the shorter it is the better it is in agreement with this exercise of the spirit. Such a one is the word 'God' or the word 'love.'"

The ancient prayer form suggested by *The Cloud* has been renewed and interpreted for our time through the centering prayer movement. As developed by its principal teachers, this contemplative practice involves several basic steps: At the beginning of prayer we turn in faith to the God dwelling in our depths. Then we take up a short word and let it repeat itself silently within. The word usually drops away as we allow ourselves simply to open to God's love. Whenever in the course of our prayer we find ourselves aware of other thoughts, we gently return to the word, letting it anchor us in the divine Presence. It is recommended that we center for about twenty minutes, twice a day if possible, and close with a familiar prayer.

The fruits of this prayer do not reside in the subjective feelings we experience during it—comfort, frustration, peace, discouragement—but in the slow transformation it works in our lives. The touchstone for centering prayer, as for all contemplation, is found in the letter to the Ephesians: "I pray that you may have the power to comprehend, with all the saints, what is the breadth and length and height and depth, and to know the love of Christ that surpasses knowledge, so that you may be filled with all the fullness of God" (3:18–19).

Centering prayer dispenses with images, but other forms of prayer rely on speech and the imagination, especially in dark times. Intercessory prayer has always been a spontaneous human response to the experience of darkness. With the psalmist we instinctively cry out: "Help me, O LORD my God! Save me according to your steadfast love" (Ps 109:26). Jesus refers often to this type of prayer and engages in it himself, but many Christians still feel conflicted about prayer that asks God to do something. They wonder, along with much traditional theology, whether prayer really changes or influences God's interaction with the world, or simply brings about a change in the person who prays. Further, they suspect that intercession may be a less perfect way of praying, born of need and failure.

Contemporary understandings of the universe as dynamic and relational illumine these dilemmas. In such a world, intercessory prayer does indeed matter to the person praying and to all other creatures. And it also makes a difference even to God that we pray in this way. In an interdependent world, we affect God by what we are, feel, and do. The twentieth-century philosopher and mathematician Alfred North Whitehead calls God the *fellow sufferer who understands*, and *final wisdom*. God's love is compassionate, taking the world's experience into the divine experience, suffering with its sufferings and rejoicing with its joys. These events are transformed in the divine freedom and then influence God's ongoing guidance of the world. God takes account of human prayers, even though in their initial form they may not be compatible with the breadth of divine purpose and must be reshaped in its love. They open up new possibilities for the divine dialogue with creation in its next moment of existence. In dark times they become especially important ways of bringing about change in the universe.

Such belief in the power of prayer fueled Thomas Merton's struggle against the evils threatening civilization. In his *Cold War Letters*, Merton addressed a cultural impasse similar to our own and described the paradox of finding God's presence in a dark spiritual landscape. In his letters from October 1961 to October 1962, the year leading up to the Cuban missile crisis, Merton warns that the survival of the entire human race is at stake in the imminent threat of nuclear war, and he pleads with Christians to act while there is still time. Merton regards our willingness to risk killing everyone and everything on earth as "purely and simply the crucifixion all over again." Our survival depends, he believes, on the seemingly impossible goal of transforming the hearts and minds of millions of people across the world. At the edge of the abyss, when all seems lost, he believes that prayer holds the power to bring about such change. So in the midst of what he saw as total darkness, Merton continued to write letters that speak prophetically to us today, attempting to evoke God's presence in each of his correspondents and relying on the power of prayer to bring about the kind of global conversion necessary to avert disaster.

CHAPTER 12

A LEGACY FOR
FUTURE GENERATIONS

Lord, make this world to last as long as possible.

—Prayer of an Eleven-Year-Old Child

In 587 BCE, Babylonian troops captured the beloved city of Jerusalem and burned all its buildings, including the temple constructed by Solomon to house Yahweh's special presence. The city's leaders, priests, and sages were forced to walk hundreds of miles to live as aliens amid their captors in the land of Babylon. The opening lines of Psalm 137 disclose the despair felt by these exiles: "By the rivers of Babylon—there we sat down and there we wept when we remembered Zion."

As the decades pass, the exiles—now bereft of family, friends, homeland, and perhaps even their God—sink deeper into hopelessness. Then a prophet appears among them who invokes a very old memory.

> Listen to me, you that pursue righteousness,
> you that seek the LORD.
> Look to the rock from which you were hewn,
> and to the quarry from which you were dug.
> Look to Abraham your father
> and to Sarah who bore you.... (Isa 51:1–2a)

Isaiah speaks to grandparents and grandchildren, parents and children, to those who remember Jerusalem and to others for whom the walls and canals of Babylon comprise all they have ever known. Deep in the midst of exile, the prophet calls on memory to create a community of hope; he lifts up ancient stories to ground the possibility of a joyous homecoming. Isaiah evokes Sarah, once considered barren, who laughs at impossibility and gives birth to the future. He uses the days of Noah to serve as a reminder that God's faithful love will prevail even in the present chaos.

> For the mountains may depart
> and the hills be removed,
> but my steadfast love shall not depart from you,
> and my covenant of peace shall not be removed,
> says the LORD, who has compassion on you.
> (Isa 54:10)

From these ancient traditions an exiled people learns that its deepest longings will be fulfilled through God's promises and their own response across the generations. But in order to move forward, they must know their lineage. The hopes of past, present, and future generations are intrinsically linked.

This biblical pattern of drawing on the past to shape a legacy for those yet to come remains fundamental to the covenant between the generations. We need these intergenerational commitments today more than ever, when the dreams of children and grandchildren throughout the world are threatened by cynicism and hopelessness. A mother sitting on a rock as her young daughter plays in the ocean nearby puts it simply: "I want to do something about the threats to our planet for my kids' sake; I want them to have something of the world I know." Love of our children and grandchildren—of children throughout the universe—is one of the most compelling motives for preserving life on Earth.

We can no longer assume that future generations will enjoy the same landscapes and seasons, oceans and skies, animals and plants as those who came before them. Already they will inherit a greatly altered biosphere. Concern for the kind of world we are leaving these next generations can sustain action on behalf of the Earth community. Several themes from Christian spirituality strengthen this awareness of our responsibility for the survival and well-being of our descendants around the globe.

THE MEANING OF VOCATION IN THIS HISTORICAL MOMENT

A deep hunger for spiritual experience lives beneath the surface of our wired world. When envisioning such experience, however, we may imagine that it consists of personal consolation and comfort, visions and voices, or even miraculous interventions. We are not entirely prepared for the way a genuine encounter with God moves us to action. But from biblical and historical figures, we learn that spiritual experience does not end in ecstasy and rapture but moves its recipients to vocation and mission. It not only brings joy and strength; it asks something of us.

We see this preeminently in Jesus. His union with the Father fueled a passionate mission to free the hungry, the sick, the poor, sinners, lepers, and prostitutes—all the lost, the last, and the miserable. Jesus lived in a time like our own, when it seemed that the world was about to end. Many of his Jewish contemporaries were convinced that they teetered on the brink of an apocalyptic catastrophe. Into this context Jesus brought hope for a future rooted in divine presence and promise.

A similar convergence of divine presence and mission occurs in the experience of Jesus' disciples. Mary of Nazareth emerges from her encounter with an angelic visitor with a firm commitment to the role she is asked to play in the salvation of future generations. Her Magnificat is filled with references to ancestors and descendants, and with appreciation for the contributions each generation makes to the good news of salvation: "Surely, from now on all generations will call me blessed; / for the Mighty One has done great things for me..." (Luke 1:48–49).

We also see how mission issues from sacred encounter in the story of Mary Magdalene's early morning meeting with the risen Jesus. Overcome with anguish when she discovers that his body is missing from the tomb, Mary recovers her deep relationship with Jesus when he speaks her name in the garden. But Jesus directs her desire for union with him to the community of his disciples, the new locus of his presence in the world. As witness to the paschal events, she moves immediately into apostolic action: "Mary Magdalene went and announced to the disciples, 'I have seen the Lord'" (John 20:18).

We too find a vocation or call embedded in our experiences of the divine presence. This vocation may concern matters large or small and take shape only gradually, but it stems from the dynamics of love—we come to care about, and want to bring about, what matters to the persons we love. This call impelled Israel's prophets to deliver a word they hoped would make God's vision for future generations a reality, and it led the disciples of Jesus to work toward the kind of community he envisioned. Jesus left his early followers no blueprints for the venture they undertook. Nor do we have clear directives for the enormous task of developing new ways of relating to the Earth. Like Jesus' disciples, we must rely on the Spirit as we grope to find our way. But as with Mary of Nazareth, future generations will bless our willingness to birth a new age.

Thomas Berry offers a focus for our vocation at this critical moment in Earth's history. As Berry has studied the magnitude of the problems facing the human community, he has become convinced that we need a new mythic story, one that will tie our human venture to the larger destinies of the universe and heal our alienation from the Earth. Berry finds such an epic story in the evolution of the universe and the Earth: "Such a fantastic universe, with its great spiraling galaxies, its supernovas, our solar system, and this privileged planet Earth!" He believes this comprehensive narrative will orient us toward the *great work* of our time, that of creating the conditions for the flourishing of the Earth community.

In developing his idea of the *new story*, Berry was strongly influenced by the work of Teilhard de Chardin. From Teilhard he came to appreciate how human experience is situated within a cosmos gradually unfolding across an immense sweep of geological time. He also drew from Teilhard the conviction that some form of consciousness or interiority is present in the process of evolution from the beginning. Matter is numinous, comprised of both a spiritual and a physical dimension. Consciousness thus exists in all life forms, but in different ways. In human beings, the consciousness that links all life becomes self-consciousness or reflective thought. As self-reflective beings, we have a special responsibility for the future of the universe. It is our actions, for example, that will determine which species survive and which become extinct.

According to Berry, the values and actions we need today flow from a basic understanding of the universe. Three processes are key to this new perspective: differentiation, or the extraordinary variety and distinctiveness of all beings in the universe; subjectivity, the interior numinous quality of all reality; and communion, the capacity to relate to all people and life forms. In a recent address on "Loneliness and Presence," Berry draws these strands together. Our intimacy with the universe, he says, includes a presence to its smallest particles as well as the vast number of stars filling the sky in all directions. We discover a more immediate presence in the Earth's landscapes, grasses, flowers, forests, and fauna. In the full range of their diversity, animals belong in our consciousness in a special way. Of these components of the universe, he says: "Each in its own distinctive perfection fills our mind, our imagination, our emotional attraction." This story of the universe lifts up communion, rather than domination and control, as the mode of human interaction with the Earth community. The vocation, or great work of our time, then, requires that we awaken to the sacred dimensions of the natural world; to the rich contributions each species brings to the whole; and to the vital, vibrant interactions among all the subjects who share life on our planet.

Elders from many traditions whose calling is to look to the future of the entire community witness to such a vocation. In John G. Neihardt's *Black Elk Speaks*, a Native American holy man recounts a vision in which he sees that the sacred hoop of his own people appears as one of many hoops that make up a larger circle. The circle is as wide as daylight and starlight. In the center grows a mighty tree that shelters all the children of one mother and one father. His vision indicates his spiritual role in his own tribe and is also a testament intended for all humankind.

In a similar vein, the Laguna Pueblo/Sioux Indian writer Paula Gunn Allen tells us in *The Sacred Hoop* of the legacy her mother left her. When she was a small child her mother taught her that all animals, insects, and plants are to be treated with respect. Life is a circle, her mother would say, in which everything has its place. Gunn learned to look to the wind and sky, the trees and rocks, the sticks and stars to teach her. These attitudes led to a sense of connection to the land and all her creatures, as well as to carefulness in the use of the Earth's resources.

A SPIRITUAL PRACTICE FOR DEFINING OUR LEGACY: THE ETHICAL WILL

The new cosmic story includes sweeping visions of the universe that, like a star-studded night sky, evoke wonder and expand perspectives. However, they can also make our contributions seem insignificant by comparison. A passage from Marilyn Robinson's Pulitzer Prize–winning novel *Gilead* eases that feeling. In the novel, a seventy-seven-year-old Congregationalist preacher learns that his failing heart will soon stop beating, so he sets about writing a long, gentle letter for his son to read after his death. At one point in the letter he muses: "There are a thousand, thousand reasons to live this life, every one of them sufficient." Each calling is unique and valuable.

The preacher's letter that comprises *Gilead* might be considered a fictional example of an ethical will. Recently there has been a resurgence of interest in this way of leaving a spiritual legacy for those we love. An ancient practice rooted in the Bible and the Jewish Talmud, copies of ethical wills have been preserved from modern times, and also from the medieval and Renaissance periods and the Holocaust. One written by Shulamit

Rabinovitch on June 6, 1944, to her sons who had escaped to America, reads: "Dear Children, don't take foolish things to heart, be happy, contented people. Fight for freedom and social justice...and don't mourn for us with tears and words, but rather with deeds." Rabinovitch's wisdom is bequeathed to her children in the darkest of moments.

Different versions of the ethical will can be found in many cultures, but at their core, such wills offer a way to leave one's descendants something more precious than material possessions. The terms *ethical* and *spiritual* are used interchangeably to distinguish this type of document from a legal will. Through letters, videos, memoirs, or separate documents attached to legal wills, a person imparts to loved ones treasured assets such as values, stories, memories, hopes for the future, and wisdom gleaned from experience.

Although often seen as a way to bring final closure to a life—like the dying patriarch Jacob's blessing of his sons in the Book of Genesis—spiritual wills constitute a fruitful practice at any age or life period. They prove especially important during transitions such as retirement, marriage, divorce, a major illness, or the celebration of birthdays and anniversaries. Persons with early dementia compose them so that their families will remember who they were before the progression of their illness. A teacher found ethical wills especially beneficial to women in prison for life who feared they would be forgotten by their families. A client of mine who was dying of breast cancer, realizing that her two young children would long to know her better as they grew older, prepared a letter telling them about her own childhood, her beliefs and regrets, and her love and hopes for them.

There are no set rules for writing an ethical will. People choose whatever length and style they wish—a single page, a longer memoir, a history of their heritage, or an explanation of why they are leaving money to support a particular cause. Ethical wills are often addressed to specific persons and close with parting words. Although most suggestions for writing spiritual wills focus mainly on personal and family matters, it is important, in light of our current awareness of larger connections in the universe, that they be intentionally expanded to include the rest of creation as well. To incorporate this ecological perspective, a person might consider questions such as: What landscapes—desert, forest, wilderness—have shaped me, beginning with my childhood? How has nature been a source of religious meaning and spiritual experience? What animals have befriended me, and what have they taught me over the years? How has a lifelong concern for creation shaped my spiritual journey? What kind of a universe do I hope to leave you, my descendants?

A section from my own spiritual will expresses this social dimension as a bequest to those I love: "I leave to you the ten thousand flowers of spring, the forests I have loved, the mountain trails I have hiked, the ocean shores I have roamed. I will to you a world in which love and justice are seen as more powerful and effective than violence and hatred, where our differences do not divide, but enrich, us." Each of these statements tells me what I must do to bring about the inheritance I hope to bequeath to future generations. The legacy I want to leave offers more possible actions than could creatively be pursued in one lifetime.

The reading of memoirs can help to shape a legacy by suggesting ways in which nature is a part of every life story. Such literary works clarify how human life is intertwined with particular landscapes, and illumine similar connections in our own personal and family histories. In *Refuge*, the nature writer Terry Tempest Williams turns for solace and sanctuary to the birds and landscape of the Great Salt Lake as she grieves her mother's cancer and eventual death. She steps back in time to remember:

"The Bird Refuge has remained a constant. It is a landscape so familiar to me, there have been times I have felt a species long before I saw it." She ponders human mortality and that of the natural environment as well, for, as she says good-bye to her mother, she also loses her beloved birds—burrowing owls, snowy egrets, barn swallows, meadowlarks—when the Bear River Migratory Bird Refuge is covered by the rising waters of the Great Salt Lake.

Williams relates her experiences to her Mormon faith and ponders complex layers of engagement with nature, including the likely origin of her family history of breast cancer in radioactive fallout from atomic bomb tests in the Utah desert. As *Refuge* concludes, she recounts how all these interlaced events led her to an act of civil disobedience. She crossed the line at the Nevada Test Site and was arrested for trespassing. Williams calls this her gesture on behalf of all the women in her family who have died of breast cancer. When she and the other protestors are released in the desert to find their way home, she is heartened by the Joshua trees standing their ground, trees that were so named by her ancestors because they looked like prophets pointing to the Promised Land.

A SPACIOUS INHERITANCE: THE COMMUNION OF ALL THE SAINTS

When we come to appreciate our spiritual heritage—all that comes to us as grace—we more readily recognize our responsibility to succeeding generations. When Abraham is called to leave his country and kindred for an unknown destination, God tells him: "…I will bless you, and make your name great, so that you will be a blessing" (Gen 12:2). Heritage implies a debt to be paid by extending a similar gift to others. There are many avenues for doing this, but as concern for the Earth grows, we might spend our inheritance by planting trees we ourselves will never see fully grown, building alternative transportation systems we will not live long enough to ride, or preserving habitats in distant lands we will never have a chance to visit.

Leaving a legacy constitutes an act of gratitude to all those who have contributed to our person and our universe. Our individual talents have been nurtured by grandparents and parents, friends and mentors. The beauty of landscapes and oceans has been preserved by courageous figures around the globe. Our understanding of prayer drinks from wells filled by Teresa of Avila and John of the Cross. The gospel vision of simplicity lives on in the life of Francis of Assisi. Birds, fish, and grasshoppers breathe more easily because Rachel Carson fought the use of pesticides. Hope for a Beloved Community lodges in our imaginations because Martin Luther King undertook a lifelong march for justice. Houses of hospitality have sprung up across our land because Dorothy Day believed there would always be enough bread for everyone. Strands too numerous to count are woven into the mantle of our inheritance. We say thank you by preserving, amplifying, and passing on these blessings.

Through memory, a community preserves its ancient springs of wisdom and offers them as streams of hope for thirsty hearts. Theologian Mary C. Grey describes how this is especially true of peoples of the world who struggle for liberation, such as the inhabitants of Rajasthan, India. When older people in this desert region are asked to remember what their landscape looked like when they were children, they can tell of a time when trees were abundant, when wood for cooking and animal fodder could be found without long searching. They remember that they survived cyclic droughts by consuming water in proportion to its availability, like the biblical desert dwellers whose Jubilee Laws enabled them to honor the rhythm of the land's fertile and lean years. Grey notes that the people of Jaisalmer were able to survive the drought of 1987 because of their water-harvesting structures. This is no longer possible due to inappropriate management of water supplies, excessive demands for water, and the lost memory of traditional methods of water conservation.

The tapestry of holiness fashioned from past, present, and future is encompassed by the ancient symbol of the communion of saints. When we think of saints, the figures that initially come to mind are those the church commemorates during the liturgical year, remembering their contributions and invoking their ongoing care through celebrations and litanies. Recently the ecological significance of many of these saints has been rediscovered.

The thirteenth-century Dominican philosopher and theologian Albert the Great is one example of this search for inspiration from the saints' attitudes toward the cosmos. Albert's historical fame often rests on his role as teacher of Thomas Aquinas, but he also pioneered as a natural scientist. In the Middle Ages, his efforts in physics, astronomy, chemistry, zoology, and botany earned comparisons to Aristotle. A mendicant priest, Father Albert traveled about western Europe by foot, studying local animals, flowers, and vegetation and inquiring about them of residents in the villages and mountains. It is said that he once had himself lowered over the edge of a cliff to see whether eagles truly do lay only one egg each season, as was commonly thought to be the case. Though at times criticized for his scientific interests, Albert considered them a way of coming to know and serve the Creator. Because of his dedication to the pursuit of wisdom in all its forms, he became the patron of both philosophers and scientists.

More recently, the communion of saints has been enriched by the life of the American-born Notre Dame de Namur Sister Dorothy Stang. In 1966 Dorothy began a ministry to the poor and landless peasants of Brazil, teaching them small-scale sustainable agriculture and working for land reform. She made her home in the town of Anapu, on the edge of the vast Para region of the Amazon rain forest, and received increasing death threats for confronting the illegal logging firms and ranchers who were destroying the rain forest. In February of 2005, as she traveled into the jungle to a meeting of small farmers and peasants, Dorothy was confronted by hired gunmen. She opened her Bible and began reading to them from the Beatitudes. They listened for a moment and then shot her six times. The local people called Dorothy "Dora," or "the angel of the Trans-Amazonian." After her brutal death, she became known as the Martyr of the Amazon; her courage continues to inspire those working for justice for the Earth and all its peoples.

Although certain saints figure prominently in our litanies and liturgies, the communion of saints does not refer primarily to those officially declared saints. It applies first of all to the whole community made one by the indwelling of God. As theologian Elizabeth A. Johnson understands it, this symbol stands most fundamentally for the intergenerational company of persons who have been touched by the Holy and who share as well in the sacredness of the entire cosmos. This community of life—past, present, and future—relies on Sophia for its connections and holiness. In the Book of Wisdom we learn that "in every generation she passes into holy souls and makes them friends of God, and prophets" (7:27). The company Wisdom keeps is marked by mutuality and equality. Holiness arises everywhere, in all cultures and contexts, and we find ourselves in the presence of saints in unexpected times and places.

Traditionally, the communion of saints has referred exclusively to human persons and their relationships with one another. This definition has now been expanded to reflect the holiness found throughout creation. We are companions in the Spirit with persons and with all of nature as well—stardust, galaxies, creatures large and small. Together we exist in the deepest of communions, a unity that reflects the trinitarian God. The spark of Divine Wisdom that fires the holiness of the saints also burns in every creature in the universe. All are called to the fullness of what they can become, and all contribute their unique gifts to the whole. When we celebrate this heritage in litany and song, we bring to mind who we are and how, in the fullness of our communion, we image God. Naming the saints has taken many historical and cultural forms—lament, praise, blessings, thanksgiving, intercession. Lament expresses sorrow at sufferings endured, pain inflicted, and deeds left undone. Praise rejoices in the richness of our heritage and God's abundant creativity. Blessings pull us into the present, since they draw on the power of the immediate. Gratitude acknowledges our interdependence, for when we say thank you we recognize gifts received.

A closing litany brings together these forms of remembrance and their meaning for our own legacy:

> We lift a chorus of praise to you, Sophia,
> joining with all peoples across the globe,
> blending our speech with the voices of soft rain and
>   desert heat,
> lofty pines and jeweled frost crystals, splendid ravens
>   and soaring eagles,
> pulsating jellyfish and fragile hummingbirds,
> patient reptiles and industrious beavers, graceful elk
>   and powerful bears,
> radiant stars and spinning planets.

>   Teach us to reverence your creation.

> We repent of the losses we have inflicted on our
>   planet.
> We mourn the silenced songbirds and scorched soil,

slashed forests and polluted seas, unclean air and
vanishing bees.
We weep for those people whose lives have been
fractured and diminished, rendered intolerable
and cut short by our wars and ethnic cleansing,
our violence and our greed.
We have failed to live by your grace, and we seek
forgiveness and healing.

Teach us to reverence your creation.

We give thanks for all the saints who have inhabited
this Earth before us,
from whose lives our own faith has been fashioned.
We are filled with gratitude for these ancestors who
learned to abide in you,
and there found courage to dream the dreams and see
the visions
now bequeathed to us as heritage and hope.

Teach us to reverence your creation.

Bless all living beings now making their way in your
universe,
all creatures who embrace and uphold us,
who show us our unique gifts in time and space,
who add to our particular pattern and presence.
Bless peoples of every race and religion, every gender
and difference,
every culture and calling, every country and nation.
Bless algae and bacteria, alpine wildflowers and
pesky mosquitoes,
cloying air and gentle breezes, penguins and puppies,
waterfalls and rivers, farmland and meadows.

Teach us to reverence your creation.

Creator Spirit, you who dwell within our cosmic chaos, infuse with fresh love all our atoms, cells, and sinews. Forgive and renew us. Convert our hearts, and turn us around again and again until we discern your face in all you have created and forge new ways of living together in your universe. Amen.

NOTES AND FURTHER READING

🌿 Scripture quotations, unless otherwise noted, are from the New Revised Standard Version, copyright 1989 by the Division of Christian Education of the National Council of the Churches of Christ in the United States of America; reprinted by permission of the publisher.

Unless otherwise indicated, the prayers, rituals, and exercises throughout the book are my own.

PREFACE

Pope John Paul II, "The Ecological Crisis: A Common Responsibility," reprinted in *This Sacred Earth: Religion, Nature, Environment*, ed. Roger S. Gottlieb (London: Routledge, 1996), 230–37.

CHAPTER 1
WHO WE ARE MEANT TO BE

Epigraph from Constance FitzGerald, "Transformation in Wisdom: The Subversive Character and Educative Power of Sophia in Contemplation," in *Carmel and Contemplation: Transforming Human Consciousness*, ed. Kevin Culligan and Regis Jordan (Washington, DC: ICS Publications, 2000), 346.

A short article published in 1967 by the historian Lynn White Jr. became well known and was a significant catalyst for subsequent discussion of the environmental beliefs and practices of the world religions. In his essay, White indicted the Christian tradition for its role in the ecological crisis, citing its anthropocentrism and the biblical view that human beings are given dominion over nature by God as fundamental contributions to the Western exploitation of nature. White called for a new theological vision. See Lynn White Jr., "The Historical Roots of Our Ecologic Crisis," *Science* 155 (March 10, 1967): 1203–7. The pioneering work of the following decades is summarized in the entries of *The Encyclopedia of Religion and Nature*, ed. Bron Raymond Taylor (Bristol, UK: Thoemmes Press, 2005).

In *God for a Secular Society: The Public Relevance of Theology* (Minneapolis: Fortress, 1999), 113–16, Jürgen Moltmann describes the sabbath, rather than humanity, as the goal of creation. The sabbath rest is the heart of creation's movement and meaning.

Elizabeth A. Johnson captures the meaning and power of biblical wisdom imagery for both the Jewish and Christian communities in *She Who Is: The Mystery of God in Feminist Theological Discourse* (New York: Crossroad, 1992), 124–87. See also Dianne Bergant, *Israel's Wisdom Literature: A Liberation-Critical Reading of the Old Testament* (Minneapolis: Augsburg Fortress, 1997), in which Bergant uses the integrity of creation as her interpretive lens; and James G. D. Dunn,

Christology in the Making: A New Testament Inquiry into the Origins of the Doctrine of the Incarnation, 2nd ed. (Grand Rapids, MI: Wm. B. Eerdmans, 2003).

The response to the beauty of God's presence in mountains and valleys is Constance FitzGerald's paraphrase of John of the Cross's poetic vision in *The Spiritual Canticle* 14–15. See "Transformation in Wisdom," 333–34.

Thomas Merton, "Hagia Sophia," in *A Thomas Merton Reader*, ed. Thomas P. McDonnell (New York: Doubleday, 1974), 506–11.

Denis Edwards, *Ecology at the Heart of Faith: The Change of Heart That Leads to a New Way of Living on Earth* (Maryknoll, NY: Orbis, 2006), 55. See also his *Jesus the Wisdom of God: An Ecological Theology* (Maryknoll, NY: Orbis, 1995).

Mary Evelyn Tucker, "A Communion of Subjects and a Multiplicity of Intelligences," in *A Communion of Subjects: Animals in Religion, Science, and Ethics*, ed. Paul Waldau and Kimberly Patton (New York: Columbia University Press, 2006), 647.

Mary Midgley, "Duties Concerning Islands," in *Environmental Ethics*, ed. Robert Elliot (New York: Oxford University Press, 1995), 101.

For an excellent treatment of the history and contemporary implications of the doctrine of the Trinity, see Catherine Mowry LaCugna, "God in Communion with Us," in *Freeing Theology: The Essentials of Theology in Feminist Perspective*, ed. Catherine Mowry LaCugna (San Francisco: Harper San Francisco, 1993), 83–114; and *God for Us: The Trinity and Christian Life* (San Francisco: Harper San Francisco, 1991).

Denis Edwards's comments on *perichoresis* are in *Ecology at the Heart of Faith*, 73.

Sally McFague develops the image of the world as God's body in *The Body of God: An Ecological Theology* (Minneapolis:

Fortress, 1993). In *A New Climate for Theology: God, the World, and Global Warming* (Minneapolis: Fortress, 2008), McFague focuses on climate change and the urgency of moving from an individualist, consumer anthropology to one that highlights our interdependence with all other human beings and life forms.

Thomas Berry, "Loneliness and Presence," in *A Communion of Subjects: Animals in Religion, Science, and Ethics*, 8. Berry has expressed this point in various ways in his numerous works.

Susan Griffin, *Women and Nature: The Roaring Inside Her* (New York: Harper & Row, 1978), 227.

In my book *Reclaiming the Connections: A Contemporary Spirituality* (Kansas City: Sheed & Ward, 1990), I develop further the meaning of a relational self as understood in process thought. For the dynamics of this view of the interconnectedness of all reality, see Alfred North Whitehead, *Process and Reality*, corrected edition, ed. David Ray Griffin and Donald W. Sherburne (New York: Macmillan, 1978); *Religion in the Making* (New York: Fordham University Press, 1996); and *Science in the Modern World* (New York: Macmillan, 1967).

Denis Edwards also comments on the difficulty of identifying human uniqueness with self-consciousness. He finds the *imago Dei* in the nature of human beings as personal and interpersonal, in that way emphasizing the relational nature of this uniqueness. See *Ecology at the Heart of Faith*, 15–17. Ernst M. Conradie provides a helpful analysis of approaches to human uniqueness in *An Ecological Christian Anthropology: At Home on Earth?* (Burlington, VT: Ashgate, 2005), 79–182.

Catherine Keller, *Face of the Deep: A Theology of Becoming* (New York: Routledge, 2003), 7.

Bernard M. Loomer contrasts unilateral and relational power and shows how fully Jesus embodies the relational power of love in "Two Kinds of Power," *Criterion* 15/1 (Winter 1976): 5–19.

The comment on saving African wildlife is from Raymond Bonner, *At the Hands of Man: Peril and Hope for Africa's Wildlife* (New York: Knopf, 1993), 286. See also Roger S. Gottlieb, "Spiritual Deep Ecology and the Left: An Attempt at Reconciliation," in *This Sacred Earth: Religion, Nature, Environment*, 516–31.

Arnold Benz, *The Future of the Universe: Chance, Chaos, God?* (New York: Continuum, 2000), 106 and 157.

Alfred North Whitehead, *Process and Reality*, 346, 351.

In "Transformation in Wisdom," 306–8, Constance FitzGerald reflects further on how the presence of another changes the image we have of ourselves.

Mark Wallace, "The Wounded Spirit as the Basis for Hope," in *Christianity and Ecology: Seeking the Well-Being of Earth and Humans*, ed. Dieter T. Hessel and Rosemary Radford Ruether (Cambridge, MA: Harvard University Press, 2000), 51–72. On the Spirit as the bond of mutual love, the *vinculum caritatis* or *vinculum Trinitatis*, see 56–57.

Walter Brueggemann discusses Exodus and the sabbath in *The Land: Place as Gift, Promise, and Challenge in Biblical Faith* (Philadelphia: Fortress, 1977), 34–35.

CHAPTER 2
WE WILL SAVE WHAT WE LOVE

Epigraph from *St. Hildegard of Bingen: Symphonia: A Critical Edition of the Symphonia Armonie Celestium Revelationum*, trans. and ed. Barbara Newman (Ithaca, NY: Cornell University Press, 1988), 140–41.

On the book of nature, see Constant J. Mews, "The World of the Text: The Bible and the Book of Nature in Twelfth-Century Theology," in *Scripture and Pluralism: Reading the*

Bible in the Religiously Plural Worlds of the Middle Ages and the Renaissance, ed. Thomas J. Heffernan and Thomas E. Burman (Boston: Brill, 2005), 95–122. Elizabeth A. Johnson analyzes shifting perspectives on nature in "Losing and Finding Creation in the Christian Tradition," in *Christianity and Ecology*, 3–21.

Thomas Berry makes this analysis, among other places, in his foreword to *Thomas Merton, When the Trees Say Nothing: Writings on Nature*, ed. Kathleen Deignan (Notre Dame: Sorin Books, 2003), 18–19.

Pierre Teilhard de Chardin, *The Divine Milieu* (New York: Harper & Row, 1960), 131. Teilhard's wartime experiences are covered in *The Making of a Mind: Letters from a Soldier-Priest 1914–1919* (New York: Harper & Row, 1965); and *Writings in Time of War* (New York: Harper & Row, 1968). See also Ursula King, *Spirit of Fire: The Life and Vision of Teilhard de Chardin* (Maryknoll, NY: Orbis, 1996).

Pierre Teilhard de Chardin, "The Mass on the World," in *The Hymn of the Universe* (New York: Harper & Row, 1969), 23–24. See also Mary C. Grey, "Cosmic Communion: A Contemporary Reflection on the Eucharistic Vision of Teilhard de Chardin," *Ecotheology* 10 (2005): 165–80.

"St. Patrick's Breastplate," trans. Kuno Meyer, in John O'Donohue, *Anam Cara: A Book of Celtic Wisdom* (New York: HarperCollins, 1997), 4. The second Celtic prayer is from *Carmina Gadelica*, ed. Alexander Carmichael (Edinburgh: Scottish Academic Press, 1976), III, 33. See also Esther De Waal, *The Celtic Way of Prayer: The Recovery of the Religious Imagination* (New York: Doubleday, 1997).

Belden C. Lane tells the story of the Talmudic sage in *The Solace of Fierce Landscapes: Exploring Desert and Mountain Spirituality* (New York: Oxford University Press, 1998), 189.

Julian of Norwich, *Showings*, trans. Edmund Colledge and James Walsh (New York/Mahwah, NJ: Paulist Press, 1978), Long Text, chapter 5, 183.

Jane Kenyon, "Now That We Live," and "Let Evening Come," in *Otherwise: New and Selected Poems* (Saint Paul, MN: Graywolf Press, 1996), 55, 176. Joyce Peseroff discusses Kenyon's poetic vision in "The Luminous Particular," in *Women's Review of Books*, 23/5 (September/October 2006): 22–23.

Gerard Manley Hopkins, "God's Grandeur," "Pied Beauty," and "Hurrahing in Harvest," in *Poems and Prose of Gerard Manley Hopkins*, ed. W. H. Gardner (Baltimore: Penguin, 1953), 27, 30, 31. Hopkins describes the bluebell on p. 120.

Fiona Bowie and Oliver Davies, eds., *Hildegard of Bingen: Mystical Writings*, trans. Robert Carver (New York: Crossroad, 1990), 93.

"The Importance of the Whale in the Field of Iris" and "In General," in Pattiann Rogers, *Firekeeper: Selected Poems*, 2nd ed. (Minneapolis: Milkweed Editions, 2005), 82, 240; and "Counting What the Cactus Contains," in *Song of the World Becoming: Poems, New and Collected, 1981–2001* (Minneapolis: Milkweed Editions, 2001), 136. The Pattiann Rogers interview can be found at: home.comcast.net/-yake/opn.pattiann.htm.

The story by Steve Rushin is reprinted on the Marquette University alumni Web site for June 2007: muconnect@mu.edu.

CHAPTER 3
THE WORTH OF A SINGLE SPARROW

Epigraph from Thomas Merton, *When the Trees Say Nothing: Writings on Nature*, ed. Kathleen Deignan (Notre Dame: Sorin, 2003), 49.

Edward O. Wilson details the loss of species in *The Creation: An Appeal to Save Life on Earth* (New York: Norton, 2006).

For information on the trumpeter swan and other bird populations, including ways to reverse their decline, see Jeffrey V. Wells, *Birder's Conservation Handbook: 100 North American Birds at Risk* (Princeton: Princeton University Press, 2007).

In "Is the Wild Ox Willing to Serve You?" Norman C. Habel shows how Job 38–39 challenges the mandate to dominate creation found in Genesis 1:26–28. See *The Earth Story in Wisdom Traditions*, ed. Norman C. Habel and Shirley Wurst (Cleveland: Pilgrim, 2001), 179–89. Moshe Greenberg makes the same point as he interprets Job's poetry in *The Literary Guide to the Bible*, ed. Robert Alter and Frank Kermode (Cambridge: Harvard University Press, 1987), 283–304.

A fine discussion of ethical questions related to animals, including animal consciousness, animal agency, justice for animals, pastoral ethics versus factory farming, and the use of laboratory animals, can be found in *A Communion of Subjects: Animals in Religion, Science and Ethics*. See also Jeffrey G. Sobosan, *Bless the Beasts: A Spirituality of Animal Care* (New York: Crossroad, 1991); and Debra Farrington, *All God's Creatures: The Blessing of Animal Companionship* (Brewster, MA: Paraclete Press, 2006). Farrington's book includes rituals, blessings, and prayers.

The 2007 Red List of Threatened Species can be found at www.iucnredlist.org.

"Bugs Keep Planet Livable Yet Get No Respect," *New York Times* (December 21, 1993), C1.

Respect for every creature is also a theme of "Liberating Life: A Report to the World Council of Churches," reprinted in *This Sacred Earth: Religion, Nature, Environment*, ed. Roger S. Gottlieb (New York: Routledge, 1996), 251–69.

Denis Edwards presents a creative exploration of how individual creatures are redeemed in Christ, using the sparrow as an example, in *Ecology at the Heart of Faith*, 92–98. Wilson makes his appeal to religious leaders on pp. 3–8 and his point about education on pp. 130–38 of *The Creation: An Appeal to Save Life on Earth*. See also the message from twenty-four distinguished scientists, "Preserving and Cherishing the Earth: An Appeal for Joint Commitment in Science and Religion," reprinted in Carl Sagan, *Billions and Billions* (New York: Random House, 1997), 143–45.

The *Encyclopedia of Life* can be found at www.eol.org.

This interpretation of the Isaiah and Jeremiah passages is from Walter Brueggemann, "The Creatures Know!" in *The Wisdom of Creation*, ed. Edward Foley and Robert Schreiter (Collegeville, MN: Liturgical Press), 1–12.

Sandi Doughton, "Trees Giving Bizarre Clues," *Seattle Times* (November 27, 2007): A1 and 14. Larry L. Rasmussen includes a lovely meditation on trees in *Earth Community, Earth Ethics* (Maryknoll, NY: Orbis, 1996), 208–19.

Celia Deane-Drummond presents further insights into the wisdom required for ecological decision making in *Wonder and Wisdom: Conversations in Science, Spirituality and Theology* (Radnor, PA: Templeton Foundation Press, 2006), 222–32. Deane-Drummond focuses on wisdom's roots in charity, and the importance of the four cardinal virtues of prudence, justice, fortitude, and temperance.

For a reading of Psalm 104 in diverse cultural contexts, see Arthur Walker-Jones, "Psalm 104: A Celebration of the *Vanua*"; and Abotchie Ntreh, "The Survival of Earth: An African Reading of Psalm 104," in *The Earth Story in the Psalms and the Prophets*, ed. Norman C. Habel (Cleveland: Pilgrim, 2003), 84–108. Helpful insights on incorporating the psalms into prayer can be found in *Psalms in Community: Jewish and Christian*

Textual, Liturgical, and Artistic Traditions, ed. Harold W. Attridge and Margot E. Fassler (Atlanta: Society of Biblical Literature, 2003). New translations remove one barrier to praying the psalms by offering nonsexist versions for private and communal use.

CHAPTER 4
THE DIVINE FACE IN ALL FACES

Epigraph from Catherine Keller, *Face of the Deep*, 7.

Ivone Gebara, *Longing for Running Water: Ecofeminism and Liberation* (Minneapolis: Augsburg Fortress, 1999), v–ix and 1–2.

A fine discussion of the history and current significance of the common good tradition can be found in David Hollenbach, *The Common Good and Christian Ethics* (Cambridge, UK: University of Cambridge Press, 2002); and *Modern Catholic Social Teaching: Commentaries and Interpretations*, ed. Kenneth R. Himes, et al. (Washington, DC: Georgetown University Press, 2005). For Catholics in Alliance for the Common Good, see www.catholicsinalliance.org.

United States Conference of Catholic Bishops, "Renewing the Earth: An Invitation to Reflection and Action on the Environment," "Catholic Social Teaching and Environmental Ethics," "Global Climate Change: A Plea for Dialogue, Prudence and the Common Good," and "Faithful Stewards of God's Creation: A Catholic Resource for Environmental Justice" (Washington, DC: USCC, 1991–2007). Also available at www.usccb.org.

The findings of the United Nations Intergovernmental Panel on Climate Change have been widely disseminated. The full reports of the three working groups and the Synthesis Report are available on the IPCC Web site: www.ipcc.ch, or can be purchased in book form from Cambridge University Press.

Gemma Tulud Cruz offers a fine analysis of migration as well as the call to solidarity and hospitality in "One Bread, One Body, One People: The Challenges of Migration to Theological Reflection," *Proceedings of the Catholic Theological Society of America* 62 (2007): 208–28.

Richard Elliot Friedman, *The Hidden Face of God* (New York: HarperCollins, 1995), 69.

Catherine of Siena, *The Dialogue*, trans. Suzanne Noffke (New York/Mahwah, NJ: Paulist Press, 1980), no. 7, p. 36; and no. 148, p. 311.

Merton's letter to the Sufi scholar Aziz Ch. Abdul is quoted in Michael Mott, *The Seven Mountains of Thomas Merton* (Boston: Houghton Mifflin, 1984), 433.

Thomas Merton, *New Seeds of Contemplation* (New York: New Directions, 1962), 65.

The Collected Works of St. John of the Cross, rev. ed., trans. Kieran Kavanaugh and Otilio Rodriguez (Washington, DC: Institute of Carmelite Studies, 1991), *The Dark Night*, book 1, chapter 10, no. 6.

Mary Evelyn Tucker provides an excellent discussion of the history of globalization and its intersection with ecological concerns in "Globalization and the Environment," in *Globalization and Catholic Social Thought: Present Crisis, Future Hope*, ed. John A. Coleman and William F. Ryan (Maryknoll, NY: Orbis, 2005), 87–112.

The struggle of Latin American Catholics to preserve their land and resources is recounted in Marilyn Berlin Snell, "Bulldozers and Blasphemy," *Sierra Magazine* (September/October, 2007).

In *Cry of Earth, Cry of Poor*, Leonardo Boff (Maryknoll, NY: Orbis, 1997) establishes the relationship between the plight of the oppressed and the Earth.

For the many connections between consumer choices and global justice, see "Clothing Our World in Justice," *Network Connection* (July/August 2007). James A. Nash offers a very helpful treatment of the theological and ethical dimensions of the current crisis in *Loving Nature: Ecological Integrity and Christian Responsibility* (Nashville: Abingdon Press, 1991).

The African prayer is from *Halleluia for the Day: An African Prayer Book*, ed. Anthony J. Gittins (Liguori, MO: Liguori/Triumph, 2002), 62.

Wilkie Au offers helpful insights into the Ignatian examen in *The Enduring Heart: Spirituality for the Long Haul* (New York/Mahwah, NJ: Paulist Press, 2000), 137–40.

CHAPTER 5
WHERE WONDER LEADS US

Epigraph from Rachel Carson, "The Real World Around Us," in *Lost Woods: The Rediscovered Writing of Rachel Carson*, ed. Linda Lear (Boston: Beacon, 1998), 163.

John Henry Cardinal Newman, *An Essay in Aid of a Grammar of Assent* (New York: Doubleday, 1955), 49–92.

A comprehensive treatment of the connection between wonder and religion can be found in Robert C. Fuller, *Wonder: From Emotion to Spirituality* (Chapel Hill: University of North Carolina Press, 2006).

For current insights on the importance of the emotions, see Antonio R. Damasio, *Descartes' Error: Emotion, Reason, and the Human Brain* (New York: Avon Books, 1994); *Looking for Spinoza: Joy, Sorrow, and the Feeling Brain* (Orlando: Harcourt

Brace, 2003); and Martha C. Nussbaum, *Upheavals of Thought: The Intelligence of Emotions* (Cambridge: Cambridge University Press, 2001). Leda Cosmides and John Tooby summarize research on emotions and motivation in "Evolutionary Psychology and the Emotions," in *Handbook of Emotions*, 2nd ed., ed. Michael Lewis and Jeannette M. Haviland-Jones (New York: Guilford, 2000), 103–11.

Elizabeth Kolbert, *Field Notes from a Catastrophe: Man, Nature, and Climate Change* (New York: Bloomsbury, 2006), 64–65, 189.

For an understanding of the way fear influences action, see Carroll Izard and Brian Ackerman, "Motivational, Organizational, and Regulatory Functions of Discrete Emotions," in *Handbook of Emotions*, 253–64. The power of fear is also illumined in Amy Frykholm, *Rapture Culture: Left Behind in American Culture* (New York: Oxford University Press, 2004).

Martha Nussbaum comments on the relationship of wonder to compassion in *Upheavals of Thought*, 53–55.

Robert Lyons and Chinua Achebe, *Another Africa* (London: Lund Humphries, 1998).

The Buddhist tale is recounted by Roger S. Gottlieb in "The Transcendence of Justice and the Justice of Transcendence: Mysticism, Deep Ecology, and Political Life," in *Mysticism and Transformation*, ed. Janet K. Ruffing (New York: Syracuse University Press, 2001), 189–90.

Denise Levertov, "Threat" and "Primary Wonder," in *Sands of the Well* (New York: New Directions, 1996), 5, 129.

Gerard Manley Hopkins, "God's Grandeur," in *Poems and Prose of Gerard Manley Hopkins*, 27.

Simone Weil, *Waiting for God* (New York: Harper Colophon, 1973), 105. See also Juan De Pascuale, "A Wonder Full Life," *Notre Dame Magazine* (September 2003): 49.

Helen Keller, *The Story of My Life* (New York: Doubleday, 1954), 314, 121. In *A Natural History of the Senses* (New York: Random House, 1990), Diane Ackerman suggests many avenues for opening the senses.

Rachel Carson, *Silent Spring* (Boston: Houghton Mifflin, 1962), 249; and *A Sense of Wonder* (New York: Harper & Row, 1956), 42–43. Richard Louv analyzes the reasons for what he perceives as a disconnect today between children and nature, and also suggests ways to remedy it, in *Last Child in the Woods: Saving Our Children from Nature-Deficit Disorder* (Chapel Hill, NC: Algonquin Books, 2005).

Ben Birnbaum shares the story about his mother in "Jerusalem Manor," *Image 55* (Fall 2007): 100–101.

Ignatius of Loyola, "The Deliberation on Poverty and Selections from the Spiritual Diary," in *Ignatius of Loyola: Spiritual Exercises and Selected Works*, ed. George E. Ganss (New York/Mahwah, NJ: Paulist Press, 1991), 251. Ganss comments on the translation of Ignatius's term *acatamiento* as "affectionate awe" on p. 443.

David Steindl-Rast, *Gratefulness the Heart of Prayer: An Approach to Life in Fullness* (New York/Mahwah, NJ: Paulist Press, 1984) is a classic work on gratitude.

For Heschel's life and contributions, see Edward K. Kaplan and Samuel H. Dresner, *Abraham Joshua Heschel: Prophetic Witness* (New Haven, CT: Yale University Press, 1998); and Edward K. Kaplan, *Spiritual Radical: Abraham Joshua Heschel in America, 1940–1972* (New Haven, CT: Yale University Press, 2007).

Heschel's discussion of religion and radical amazement, and his comments on civilization and the decline of wonder can be found in Abraham Joshua Heschel, *Man Is Not Alone* (New York: Farrar, Straus & Young, 1951), 8–17, 37.

CHAPTER 6
WHEN GRIEF GIVES WAY TO HOPE

Epigraph translation of the Pentecost Sequence is by Edward Caswall (1814–1878).

Robert Jay Lifton, *Death in Life: Survivors of Hiroshima* (Chapel Hill: University of North Carolina Press, 1991). The quotation is from "Apathy and Numbing—a Modern Temptation," in *The Meaning of Human Suffering*, ed. Flavian Dougherty (New York: Human Sciences Press, 1982), 196.

For further insight into dealing with the emotions, see Johanna Macy, "Working through Environmental Despair," in *Ecopsychology: Restoring the Earth, Healing the Mind*, ed. Theodore Roszak, Mary E. Gomes, and Allen D. Kanner (San Francisco: Sierra Club, 1995), 240–59. Also helpful is Miriam Greenspan, *Healing through the Dark Emotions: The Wisdom of Grief, Fear, and Despair* (Boston: Shambhala, 2003).

The story of the Kalahari Bushmen is told by Elizabeth Marshall Thomas, *The Old Way: A Story of the First People* (New York: Farrar, Straus & Giroux, 2006).

The mystical tale is adapted from Howard Schwartz, *Gabriel's Palace: Jewish Mystical Tales* (New York: Oxford University Press, 1993), 267. Schwartz comments on rabbinic teaching regarding prayer and a broken heart on p. 355.

Walter Brueggemann, *Praying the Psalms* (Winona, MN: St. Mary's Press, 1982), 69–70.

Robert Alter, "The Characteristics of Ancient Hebrew Poetry," in *The Literary Guide to the Bible*, 611–24. I use Alter's translation of Isaiah 26:17, p. 618.

Thomas P. Rausch summarizes the New Testament teaching on the "Kingdom of God," in *The New Dictionary of Catholic Spirituality*, ed. Michael Downey (Collegeville, MN: Liturgical Press, 1993), 584–86.

For a comprehensive treatment of the parables, see Arlund J. Hultgren, *The Parables of Jesus: A Commentary*, The Bible in Its World (Grand Rapids, MI: Eerdmans, 2000).

I explore the meaning of the imagination and its role in prayer and the parables in *The Inner Rainbow: The Imagination in Christian Life* (New York/Mahwah, NJ: Paulist Press, 1983). In *A Moral Creed for All Christians* (Minneapolis: Augsburg Fortress, 2005), Daniel C. Maguire makes a strong case for the indispensable role the affections play in action on behalf of the reign of God.

See Mary Catherine Hilkert, "Nature's Parables and the Preaching of the Gospel," in *The Wisdom of Creation*, 107–18.

Jerome L. McElroy, "The Habit of Hope," in *The Flying Island* 4/1 (Winter 1995): 15.

Warren Cornwall, "Big Oil Spill—From Streets," *Seattle Times* (December 1, 2007), B1 and 3.

Jung Mo Sung, "The Human Being as Subject: Defending the Victims," in *Latin American Liberation Theology: The Next Generation*, ed. Ivan Petrella (Maryknoll, NY: Orbis, 2005), 1–19.

I have adapted the problem-solving exercise from Sarah A. Conn, "When the Earth Hurts, Who Responds?" in *Ecopsychology: Restoring the Earth, Healing the Mind*, 169–70.

The Autobiography of Thérèse of Lisieux (Garden City, NY: Image, 1957).

By Little and By Little: The Selected Writings of Dorothy Day, ed. Robert Ellsberg (New York: Knopf, 1983), 335.

Kim McKay and Jenny Bonnin suggest small changes that make a big difference in *True Green: 100 Everyday Ways You Can Contribute to a Healthier Planet* (Washington, DC: National Geographic, 2007). A practical ecumenical resource for congregations is *Greening Congregations Handbook: Stories, Ideas, and Resources for Cultivating Creation Awareness and*

Care in Your Congregation, ed. Tanya Marcovna Barnett (Seattle, WA: Earth Ministry, 2002). The *Handbook* is available at 6512—23rd Avenue NW, Suite 317, Seattle, WA 98117, or online at: www.earthministry.org.

The communal nature of hope is explored by William Lynch in *Images of Hope: Imagination as Healer of the Hopeless* (New York: New American Library, 1965).

Paul Hawken, *Blessed Unrest: How the Largest Movement in the World Came into Being and Why No One Saw It Coming* (New York: Viking, 2007).

CHAPTER 7
WE HAVE HERE A LASTING HOME

Epigraph from Mary Oliver, "When Death Comes," in *New and Selected Poems* (Boston: Beacon, 1992), 11.

For the power of heaven as a vision of release from present suffering, see *The Book of Heaven: An Anthology of Writings from Ancient to Modern Times*, ed. Carol Zaleski and Philip Zaleski (New York: Oxford University Press, 2000).

Ernst M. Conradie analyzes current approaches to Earth as home in *An Ecological Christian Anthropology: At Home on Earth?* (Burlington, VT: Ashgate, 2005). Explorations of the metaphor of home in ecological writing include Shannon Jung, *We Are Home: A Spirituality of the Environment* (New York/Mahwah, NJ: Paulist Press, 1993); David Toolan, *At Home in the Cosmos* (Maryknoll, NY: Orbis, 2001); and Fritjof Capra and David Steindl-Rast, *Belonging to the Universe: Explorations on the Frontiers of Science and Spirituality* (San Francisco: Harper San Francisco, 1991).

Karla's story is told in Tom Smith (with Kevin and Karla Smith), *The Tattered Tapestry: A Family's Search for Peace with Bipolar Disorder* (New York: iUniverse Star, 2005).

Brian Swimme, *The Hidden Heart of the Cosmos: Humanity and the New Story* (Maryknoll, NY: Orbis, 1996), 29–30.

Ivone Gabara, *Longing for Running Water: Ecofeminism and Liberation*, 2.

Gladys Parentelli, "Latin America's Poor Women: Inherent Guardians of Life," in *Women Healing Earth: Third World Women on Ecology, Feminism, and Religion* (Maryknoll, NY: Orbis, 1996), 29–38.

My interpretation of the Book of Revelation is drawn from the research of Barbara R. Rossing, who views its message regarding Babylon and the New Jerusalem in economic and political terms. See her *The Choice Between Two Cities: Whore, Bride, and Empire in the Apocalypse* (Philadelphia: Trinity Press International, 1999). The quotation and Rossing's translation of Revelation 21:2–3 are from "River of Life in God's New Jerusalem," in *Christianity and Ecology: Seeking the Well-Being of Earth and Humans*, 215, 219.

Raymond Brown, *The Virginal Conception and Bodily Resurrection of Jesus* (New York/Mahwah, NJ: Paulist Press, 1973), 128–29.

I discuss resurrection more fully in my book *Imaging Life After Death: Love That Moves the Sun and Stars* (New York/Mahwah, NJ: Paulist Press, 2004). Helpful resources on this topic are *Resurrection: Theological and Scientific Assessments*, ed. Ted Peters, Robert John Russell, and Michael Welker (Grand Rapids, MI: Eerdmans, 2002); and Carolyn Walker Bynum, *Metamorphosis and Identity* (New York: Zone Books, 2001); and *The Resurrection of the Body* (New York: Columbia University Press, 1995).

The sapiential interpretation of John's gospel is developed by Sandra M. Schneiders in "Touching the Risen Jesus: Mary Magdalene and Thomas the Twin in John 20," *Proceedings of the Catholic Theological Society of America* 60 (2005): 13–35.

On El Salvador, see Mercedes Canas, "In Us Life Grows: An Ecofeminist Point of View," in *Women Healing Earth*, 24–28.

Beverly Roberts Gaventa, *Our Mother Saint Paul* (Louisville, KY: Westminster/John Knox, 2007). See also *The End of the World and the Ends of God: Science and Theology on Eschatology*, ed. John Polkinghorne and Michael Welker (Harrisburg, PA: Trinity Press International, 2000).

Anne Newlands, *Emily Carr: An Introduction to Her Life and Art* (Toronto: Firefly Books, 1996), 50.

The African American religious music is from Albert J. Raboteau, *Slave Religion: The "Invisible Institution" in the Antebellum South* (New York: Oxford University Press, 1978), 259; George Rawick, *The American Slave: A Composite Autobiography* (Westport, CT: Greenwood, 1977), vol 4: *Texas*, 6–7; and Katie Geneva Cannon, "Surviving the Blight," in *Inheriting Our Mothers' Gardens: Feminist Theology in Third World Perspective*, ed. Letty M. Russell, et al. (Philadelphia: Westminster, 1988), 75–90. Hans A. Baer and Merrill Singer discuss the themes found in this music in *African American Religion: Varieties of Protest and Accommodation*, 2nd ed. (Knoxville: University of Tennessee Press, 2002), 248–58.

Teilhard expresses this hope for the world in many of his works. See, for example, *The Hymn of the Universe*.

The promise found in creation has been a key theme of theologian John F. Haught. He develops it in *The Promise of Nature* (New York/Mahwah, NJ: Paulist Press, 1993); and "What If Theologians Took Evolution Seriously?" *New Theology Review* 18/4 (November 2005): 10–20.

CHAPTER 8
CONTEMPLATION AND
THE CARE OF CREATION

Epigraph from Thomas Berry's "Foreword" to *Thomas Merton, When the Trees Say Nothing: Writings on Nature*, ed. Kathleen Deignan (Notre Dame: Sorin Books, 2003), 19.

Evelyn Underhill, *Mysticism: A Study in the Nature and Development of Man's Spiritual Consciousness* (London: Methuen, 1911). For a selection of Underhill's works, see *Evelyn Underhill: Modern Guide to the Ancient Quest for the Holy*, ed. Dana Greene (Albany: State University of New York Press, 1988). An excellent discussion of Underhill's life and writings can be found in Dana Greene, *Evelyn Underhill: Artist of the Infinite Life* (New York: Crossroad, 1990).

The description of receptive and active modes of awareness is from Arthur J. Diekmann, "Deautomatization and the Mystic Experience," *Psychiatry* 29 (1966): 324–88. In *The Moral Context of Pastoral Care* (Philadelphia: Westminster, 1976), theologian and psychologist of religion Don Browning explains how creative adaptation requires both of these basic modalities; the active mode becomes destructive if not continuously balanced by the receptive mode. Robert Fuller offers additional avenues for distinguishing these forms of awareness in *Wonder: From Emotion to Spirituality*.

Anne Benvenuti, "Love Dogs," in *Presence: An International Journal of Spiritual Direction* 13/4 (December 2007): 30.

The Hasidic tale, "The Precious Prayer," is adapted from Howard Schwartz, *Gabriel's Palace: Jewish Mystical Tales*, 86–87.

For a classic discussion of the *apophatic* and *kataphatic* paths, see Harvey D. Egan, "Christian Apophatic and Kataphatic Mysticisms," *Theological Studies*, 39/3 (September 1978):

399–426. See also *Light from Light: An Anthology of Christian Mysticism*, 2nd ed., ed. Louis Dupré and James A. Wiseman (New York/Mahwah, NJ: Paulist Press, 2001).

The Cloud of Unknowing, ed. James Walsh, Classics of Western Spirituality (New York/Mahwah, NJ: Paulist Press, 1981).

Thomas Merton, *Contemplative Prayer* (New York: Doubleday, 1971), 30–31.

Thelma Hall offers a helpful introduction to *lectio* in *Too Deep for Words: Rediscovering Lectio Divina* (New York/Mahwah, NJ: Paulist Press, 1988). The Marmion schema is on p. 44. See also Christine Valters Paintner and Lucy Wynkoop, *Lectio Divina: Contemplative Awakening and Awareness* (New York/Mahwah, NJ: Paulist Press, 2008).

Brother Lawrence of the Resurrection, *The Practice of the Presence of God* (Old Tappan, NJ: Revell, 1958).

Chet Raymo, *Natural Prayers* (Saint Paul, MN: Hungry Mind Press, 1999), xiv–xv. Judy Cannato suggests ways to bring the new cosmology into our prayer in *Radical Amazement: Contemplative Lessons From Black Holes, Supernovas, and Other Wonders of the Universe* (Notre Dame: Sorin Books, 2006).

For the influence of the new cosmology on interpreting and directing the Ignatian *Spiritual Exercises*, see chapter 4 of Katherine Dyckman, Mary Garvin, and Elizabeth Liebert, *The Spiritual Exercises Reclaimed: Uncovering Liberating Possibilities for Women* (New York/Mahwah, NJ: Paulist Press, 2001), 85–112.

CHAPTER 9
THE TRANSFORMATION OF DESIRE

Epigraph from Wendy Farley, *The Wounding and Healing of Desire* (Louisville, KY: Westminster John Knox, 2005), xvii–xviii.

The Collected Works of St. Teresa of Avila, trans. Kieran Kavanaugh and Otilio Rodriguez, 3 vols. (Washington, DC: ICS, 1976–85). See also Carole Slade, *St. Teresa of Avila: Author of a Heroic Life* (Berkeley: University of California Press, 1995); and Alison Weber, *Teresa of Avila and the Rhetoric of Femininity* (Princeton: Princeton University Press, 1990).

Saint Augustine of Hippo, *The Confessions* (New York: Penguin, 1961), 1:1 and 4:14. Ann Belford Ulanov also illumines what we live for, and what we love, in *The Unshuttered Heart: Opening Aliveness/Deadness in the Self* (Nashville, TN: Abingdon, 2007).

For his discussion of the experience of God, see Karl Rahner, *The Practice of Faith: A Handbook of Contemporary Spirituality* (New York: Crossroad, 1983), 57–83.

Mary C. Grey, *Sacred Longings: The Ecological Spirit and Global Culture* (Minneapolis: Augsburg Fortress, 2004), 35–36.

Rebecca Mead, *One Perfect Day: The Selling of the American Wedding* (Baltimore: Penguin, 2007).

The Center for a New American Dream is a nonprofit organization whose mission is to encourage the kind of responsible consumption that will protect the environment, enhance quality of life, and promote social justice. It is located in Takoma Park, Maryland, and provides numerous practical resources, including help with parenting, on its Web site: www. newdream.org.

On the many aspects of desire and discernment, see *Ignatius of Loyola: Spiritual Exercises and Selected Works*. Helpful perspectives can also be found in Wilkie Au and Noreen Cannon, *The Discerning Heart: Exploring the Christian Path* (New York/Mahwah, NJ: Paulist Press, 2006), 133ff; and Philip Sheldrake, "Befriending Our Desires," *The Way: Review of Contemporary Christian Spirituality* 35/2 (April 1995): 91–100.

The description of peace is from Alfred North Whitehead, *Adventures of Ideas* (New York: Macmillan, 1961), 284–96.

Karl Rahner's comment on the grace of the ordinary is from *Belief Today* (New York: Sheed and Ward, 1967), 14. For his description of the mystical dimension of life, see "Everyday Mysticism," and "Experiencing the Spirit," in *The Practice of Faith*, 69–70, and 77–84.

Rich Heffern captures the power and importance of simplicity in *Adventures in Simple Living* (New York: Crossroad, 2005).

This version of the Zen tale, "Giving the Moon," is from Heather Forest, *Wisdom Tales from Around the World* (Little Rock, AR: August House, 1996), 44.

CHAPTER TEN
A NEW ASCETICISM

Epigraph from David Craig, "Cleveland December," in *Mary's House: New and Selected Poems* (Ashland, OR: Idylls Press, 2007), 95.

For a helpful discussion of Francis's love of creation, as well as further reading suggestions, see Lawrence Cunningham, *Francis of Assisi: Performing the Gospel Life* (Grand Rapids, MI: Eerdmans, 2004); and Roger Sorrell, *St. Francis of Assisi and Nature* (New York: Oxford University Press, 1988).

David Craig, "The Three Companions of St. Francis," in *Mary's House: New and Selected Poems*, 8.

Francis of Assisi, "The Testament," in *Francis and Clare: The Complete Works*, trans. Regis J. Armstrong and Ignatius C. Brady (New York/Mahwah, NJ: Paulist Press, 1982), 153–58.

For an extensive ecumenical exploration of the issues, see *Asceticism*, ed. Vincent L. Wimbush and Richard Valantasis

(New York: Oxford University Press, 1995). The essay by Kallistos Ware, "The Way of the Ascetics: Negative or Affirmative?" 3–15, in which he draws on Greek Christianity for insights applicable beyond that tradition, is especially helpful on asceticism as transfiguration by the Spirit.

Lynne M. Baab summarizes historical and contemporary forms of fasting in *Fasting: Spiritual Freedom Beyond Our Appetites* (Downers Grove, IL: InterVarsity, 2006).

Eating disorders are one of the topics treated in *The Good Body: Asceticism in Contemporary Culture*, ed. Mary G. Winkler and Letha B. Cole (New Haven, CT: Yale University Press, 1994).

Erin Hoover Barnett, "Using Her Head: Plastic-bag Hats," *Seattle Times*, February 26, 2008, E2.

Some women scholars reject the idea that the cross or Christ's suffering can be redemptive. Others insist that, while paradoxical, the cross can yet be a symbol of life. Helpful contributions to this discussion can be found in Barbara E. Reid, *Taking Up the Cross: New Testament Interpretations through Latina and Feminist Eyes* (Minneapolis: Fortress, 2007); Beverly Wildung Harrison, "The Power of Anger in the Work of Love," in *Making the Connections: Essays in Feminist Social Ethics*, ed. Carol S. Robb (Boston: Beacon, 1985), 3–21; and Rosemary Radford Ruether, *Introducing Redemption in Christian Feminism* (Cleveland: Pilgrim, 2000), 95–107.

Susan Sontag, *At the Same Time: Essays and Speeches*, ed. Paolo Dilonardo and Anne Jump (New York: Farrar, Straus & Giroux, 2007).

Margaret R. Miles, *Fullness of Life: Historical Foundations for a New Asceticism* (Philadelphia: Westminster, 1981). See also her *Desire and Delight: A New Reading of Augustine's Confessions* (New York: Crossroad, 1992). Peter Robert Brown, *The Body and Society: Men, Women, and Sexual Renunciation in Early Christianity* (New York: Columbia University Press, 1988) is a classic treatment of asceticism.

The Spiritual Canticle 7.6, in *The Collected Works of St. John of the Cross.*

For Clare of Assisi, see *Francis and Clare: The Complete Works*, 189–236.

Thomas Merton, *The Wisdom of the Desert* (New York: New Directions, 1970), 3–24.

Mary Karr, "Afterword: Facing Altars: Poetry and Prayer," in *Sinners Welcome: Poems* (New York: HarperCollins, 2006), 69–93.

On asceticism as cultural protest and the importance of the alternating rhythms of renunciation and celebration, see "Practices and Meanings of Asceticism in Contemporary Religious Life and Culture: A Panel Discussion," in *Asceticism*, 588–606.

For a discussion of Hispanic celebrations and festivals, see *Alabadle: Hispanic Christian Worship*, ed. Justo L. González (Nashville: Abingdon, 1996). The quotation is from González's introduction, p. 21. Ada María Isasi-Diaz, in *Mujerista Theology: A Theology for the Twenty-First Century* (Maryknoll, NY: Orbis, 1996), describes how liturgy and ritual support Hispanic women in their struggles.

CHAPTER 11
IN A DARK TIME WE BEGIN TO SEE

Epigraph from Edith Stein, "The Hidden Life and Epiphany," in *The Hidden Life: Hagiographic Essays, Meditations, Spiritual Texts*, trans. Waltraut Stein (Washington, DC: ICS, 1992), 109.

The statistic on species extinction is from Edward O. Wilson, *The Creation: An Appeal to Save Life on Earth* (New York: Norton, 2006), 74. On wars in the twentieth century, see Niall Ferguson, *The War of the World: Twentieth-Century Conflict and the Descent of the West* (Baltimore: Penguin, 2006). Gil Baillie, in *Violence Unveiled* (New York: Crossroad, 1995), analyzes our current crisis and the need for a major cultural shift. The reflection by the Katrina volunteer is from Stuart Eskenazi, "Tales from 'This Hectic Place,'" *Seattle Times*, April 26, 2007, A14.

I am indebted to Constance FitzGerald's interpretation of our cultural dark night, "Impasse and Dark Night," in *Women's Spirituality: Resources for Christian Development*, ed. Joann Wolski Conn (New York/Mahwah, NJ: Paulist Press, 1986), 287–311.

The quotation on the loss of our usual ways of functioning is from *The Dark Night*, book I, chap. 8, no. 3, in *The Collected Works of Saint John of the Cross*. On John's life, see Kieran Kavanaugh, *John of the Cross, Doctor of Light and Love* (New York: Crossroad, 1999); and Colin Thompson, *St. John of the Cross: Songs in the Night* (Washington, DC: Catholic University of America Press, 2003).

The Spiritual Canticle 36.7 in *The Collected Works of Saint John of the Cross*. See also *Carmelite Prayer: A Tradition for the 21st Century*, ed. Keith J. Egan (New York/Mahwah, NJ: Paulist Press, 2003); and Jane Kopas, *Seeking the Hidden God* (Maryknoll, NY: Orbis, 2005).

Mother Teresa: Come Be My Light: The Private Writings of the "Saint of Calcutta," ed. Brian Kolodiejchuk (New York: Doubleday, 2007), 47–50, 105–6, 192–93, 230.

Melissa Raphael, *The Female Face of God in Auschwitz: A Jewish Feminist Theology of the Holocaust* (New York: Routledge, 2003), 7. Her envisioning of *tikkun* is on pp. 134–45.

Cormac McCarthy, *The Road* (New York: Random House, 2006), 28, 5, 75, 273, 278–79, 286. The quotations are punctuated as in the original. The relationship of *The Road* to the *via negativa* was first suggested to me by Tom Ryan in his review, "Cormac McCarthy's Catholic Sensibility," *National Catholic Reporter* (May 4, 2007): 13–14.

The Cloud of Unknowing, chapter 7, p. 134.

Thomas Keating offers a helpful introduction to centering prayer in *Open Mind, Open Heart: The Contemplative Dimension of the Gospel* (New York: Continuum, 1994). Cynthia Bourgeault shares the fruits of her teaching in *Centering Prayer and Inner Awakening* (Lanham, MD: Cowley, 2004).

Alfred North Whitehead, *Process and Reality*, 347, 351.

Thomas Merton, *Cold War Letters*, ed. Christine M. Bochen and William H. Shannon (Maryknoll, NY: Orbis), 2006.

Chapter 12
A LEGACY FOR FUTURE GENERATIONS

Epigraph from *Earth Prayers from Around the World: 365 Prayers, Poems, and Invocations for Honoring the Earth*, ed. Elizabeth Roberts and Elias Amidon (San Francisco: Harper San Francisco, 1991), 84. The child prayed on hearing of Sino-Indian border fighting.

Walter Brueggemann develops the connection between memory and hope in *Hopeful Imagination: Prophetic Voices in Exile* (Philadelphia: Fortress, 1983).

The relationship between religious experience and vocation is explored from a variety of perspectives in *Mysticism and Social Transformation*, ed. Janet K. Ruffing (New York: Syracuse University Press, 2001).

Albert Nolan convincingly describes the similarities between Jesus' time and our own in *Jesus Before Christianity*, 25th anniversary edition (Maryknoll, NY: Orbis, 2001). Thomas Berry's comments on the universe are from *The Dream of the Earth* (San Francisco: Sierra Club, 1988), xv; and *A Communion of Subjects: Animals in Religion, Science, and Ethics*, 6. See also Thomas Berry, *The Great Work: Our Way into the Future* (New York: Bell Tower, 2000). Berry's contributions are summarized by Mary Evelyn Tucker in *The Encyclopedia of Religion and Nature*, 164–66.

John G. Neihardt, *Black Elk Speaks: Being the Life Story of a Holy Man of the Oglala Sioux* (Lincoln: University of Nebraska Press, 1961), 43.

Paula Gunn Allen, *The Sacred Hoop: Recovering the Feminine in American Indian Traditions* (Boston: Beacon, 1986), 1.

Marilyn Robinson, *Gilead* (New York: Farrar, Straus & Giroux, 2004), 243.

Shulamit Rabinovitch's letter to her sons is from Rabbi Jack Riemer and Nathaniel Stampfer, *So That Your Values Will Live On: Ethical Wills and How to Prepare Them* (Woodstock, VT: Jewish Lights Publishing, 1991), 53–56. Further help with preparing ethical wills can be found in Herbert Brokering, *I Will to You: Leaving a Legacy for Those You Love* (Minneapolis: Augsburg Fortress, 2006); Barry Baines, *Ethical Wills: Putting Your Values on Paper* (Cambridge, MA: Perseus, 2001); and Rachael Freed, *Women's Lives, Women's Legacies: Passing Your Beliefs and Blessings to Future Generations* (Minneapolis: Fairview Press, 2003).

Terry Tempest Williams, *Refuge: An Unnatural History of Family and Place* (New York: Vintage Books, 1991), 21.

Richard Elliott Friedman emphasizes the debt we owe our ancestors in *The Hidden Face of God* (San Francisco: Harper San Francisco, 1995), 278–79.

Mary C. Grey, *Sacred Longings: The Ecological Spirit and Global Culture* (Minneapolis: Fortress, 2004), 43.

The meaning of the communion of saints is comprehensively explored by Elizabeth A. Johnson in *Friends of God and Prophets: A Feminist Theological Reading of the Communion of Saints* (New York: Continuum, 1998). See also the biographies, readings, hymns, and prayers in Philip H. Pfatteicher, *The New Book of Festivals and Commemorations: Toward a Common Calendar of Saints* (Minneapolis: Fortress, 2008).

Albertus Magnus, *On Animals: A Medieval Zoologica*, trans. Kenneth F. Kitchell and Irven M. Resnick (Baltimore: Johns Hopkins University Press, 1999).

Binka Le Breton, *The Greatest Gift: The Courageous Life and Martyrdom of Sister Dorothy Stang* (New York: Doubleday, 2008).

On the inclusion of the natural world in this communion of the holy, see Johnson, *Friends of God and Prophets*, 240–42. In another context, Johnson comments on an ambiguity in the original Latin term *communion sanctorum*, which would allow the natural world to be fully included. *Sanctorum* may refer either to holy persons (*sancti*), or to holy things (*sancta*); medieval theologians used both meanings. See Elizabeth A. Johnson, "Community on Earth as in Heaven: A Holy People and a Sacred Earth Together," *The Santa Clara Lectures* 5/1 (October 1998): 13. See also Belden Lane, "Open the Kingdom for a Cottonwood Tree," *Christian Century* (October 29, 1997): 979–83; and Thomas McKenna, "Saints and Ecology," *New Theology Review* (August 1994): 47–60.